THE *INSTANTIA* OF THE LAWSUIT

A Historical Conspectus and A Commentary

The Catholic University of America
Canon Law Studies
No. 371

The *Instantia* of the Lawsuit

A Historical Conspectus and a Commentary

A DISSERTATION

Submitted to the Faculty of the School of Canon Law of the Catholic University of America in Partial Fulfillment of the Requirements for the Degree of Doctor in Canon Law

BY

Rev. Albert W. Olkovikas, S.T.L., J.C.L.
Priest of the Diocese of Manchester

THE CATHOLIC UNIVERSITY OF AMERICA PRESS
WASHINGTON, D. C.
1957

Nihil Obstat:

John Rogg Schmidt, A.B., LL.B., J.C.D.
Censor Deputatus

Washingtonii, D.C., die 14 maii, 1956

Imprimatur:

✠ MATTHAEUS FRANCISCUS BRADY, D.D.
Episcopus Manchesteriensis

Manchesterii, die 16 maii, 1956

TABLE OF CONTENTS

FOREWORD ix

PART ONE

HISTORICAL CONSPECTUS

CHAPTER I

THE *LITIS INSTANTIA* DEFINED 1

Introduction 1

Article 1. The Position of the *Litis Instantia* in Judicial Procedure 1

Article 2. The *Acta Processus* and the *Acta Causae* 4

Article 3. The *Peremptio Instantiae* and the *Praescriptio Actionis* 6

CHAPTER II

THE *PEREMPTIO INSTANTIAE*: ROMAN AND ECCLESIASTICAL LAW TO THE COUNCIL OF TRENT 7

Introduction 7

Section I. Roman Law and the *Peremptio Instantiae* 8

Article 1. Some Basic Notions of Roman Procedural Law 8

Article 2. Revision under the Autocratic Empire 12

Article 3. Restoration under Justinian (527-565) 13

Section II. Influence of Roman Law in Ecclesiastical Procedure 17

Article 1. Pre-and Post-Justinian Era to the Decretals 17

Article 2. Modification and Change under the Decretals 19

A. The *Venerabilis Frater* of Honorius III 19

B. Further Commentary and Reflections on the *Venerabilis Frater* vis-à-vis the Law of *Peremptio* 21

Section III. The *Peremptio Instantiae*: Development of the Ecclesiastical Law from the Council of Trent to the Code ... 23
Article 1. The Ruling of the Council of Trent ... 23
Article 2. Diversity of Interpretation ... 24
Article 3. *Praxis Processualis* ... 26
Article 4. Significance ... 27

CHAPTER III

THE RENUNCIATION AND THE INTERRUPTION OF THE *INSTANTIA* ... 29
Section I. The Renunciation of the Instance ... 29
Article 1. Notion and Indications in Ancient Law ... 29
Article 2. Development ... 31
Section II. The Interruption of the Instance ... 34
Article 1. Notion ... 34
Article 2. Roman Jurisprudence and Development in Canonical Procedure ... 35
Article 3. Significance ... 38

PART TWO

CANONICAL COMMENTARY

CHAPTER IV

GENERAL ASPECTS OF THE *LITIS INSTANTIA* ... 39
Article 1. The Notion of the *Litis Instantia* ... 39
Article 2. The Inception of the *Litis Instantia* ... 46
Article 3. The Termination of the *Litis Instantia* ... 48

CHAPTER V

THE INTERRUPTION OF THE *LITIS INSTANTIA* ... 57
Article 1. The Notion of the Interruption of the *Litis Instantia* ... 57
Article 2. Causes Productive of the Interruption of the Instance on the Part of the Litigant ... 59
Article 3. The Interruption of the Instance on the Part of Proxies and Guardians ... 68
Article 4. Litigation over the Right to a Benefice ... 71

CHAPTER VI

THE ABATEMENT (*PEREMPTIO*) OF THE INSTANCE ... 75

Article 1. Notion of the Abatement of the Instance ... 75

Article 2. Conditions Producing the Abatement of the Instance ... 76

Article 3. Persons Affected by the Abatement of the Instance ... 81

Article 4. The Effects of the Abatement of the Instance ... 85

CHAPTER VII

THE RENUNCIATION OF THE INSTANCE AND THE ACTS OF THE PROCESS ... 91

Article 1. The Notion and Object of the Renunciation of the Instance and of the Acts of the Process ... 91

Article 2. The Formalities to be Observed in the Renunciation ... 96

Article 3. The Effects of the Renunciation ... 99

CONCLUSIONS ... 101

BIBLIOGRAPHY ... 103

ALPHABETICAL INDEX ... 109

BIOGRAPHICAL NOTE ... 115

FOREWORD

A juridically perfect and independent society has a right to govern itself independently of any other society. To do this, however, it needs not only the power to make (legislative power) and enforce (executive power) laws, but also the power to apply (judicial power) these laws to particular cases.[1] Now, the Catholic Church is such a juridically perfect and independent society. Judicial power, therefore, is an essential and integral function of the government of the Church.

The norms which govern ecclesiastical judicial procedure provide the Church with a uniform plan of applying its laws. In the one case there is substantive law, whereby the general disciplinary laws of the Church are established; in the other, adjective law, by which are insured the operation and application of these established laws. The purpose of judicial procedure is to provide such adjective law.

The concern of this treatise is directed upon the very heart of ecclesiastical judicial procedure. Until the precise matter of litigation is constituted, the actual trial of an action at law is impossible. With the precise matter in litigation determined, the actual trial begins and may progress to its conclusion. The *litis instantia* is that part of the judicial procedure which constitutes the actual trial.

The first part of the work treats of the historico-juridical development of the *litis instantia.* Of necessity, it must also treat of those elements in law which, as it were, thwart or tend to delay the successful and normal completion of the *litis instantia.* The

[1] Cf. Ottaviani, *Institutiones Iuris Publici Ecclesiastici* (3. ed., 2 vols., Civitate Vaticana: Typis Polyglottis Vaticanis, 1947-1948), I, nn. 109, 145-148, 194-195, 257-267.

scope of the historical conspectus extends from early Roman law to and through the infant years of the Church, the age of the Decretals, the period before and after the Council of Trent, and even to our day.

The second part of the work is a canonical commentary on the present law of the Church regarding the *litis instantia.* It treats of the instance of the lawsuit, first in its general aspects, and then in the specific institutes of law proper to the *litis instantia.* Thus, the proper notion of the instance of the lawsuit is established. The mutation of juridical status which may be suffered by the litigant parties is discussed together with its effect in interrupting the instance. The nature, application, and effects of the abatement of the instance *(peremptio instantiae)* and of the renunciation of the instance *(renuntiatio instantiae)* are carefully elaborated. Finally, several pertinent conclusions drawn from the research and thought expended in this study are proposed.

The writer wishes to express his gratitude to the Most Reverend Matthew Francis Brady, Bishop of Manchester, New Hampshire, for the opportunity to pursue graduate studies in Canon Law at The Catholic University of America; to the members of the Faculty of the School of Canon Law; and to all who have in any way helped in the preparation of this dissertation.

PART I
HISTORICAL CONSPECTUS

CHAPTER I
THE LITIS INSTANTIA DEFINED

Introduction

The *litis instantia* of judicial proceedings comprises those judiciary acts which begin with the joinder of issue (*litis contestatio*) and look to the completion of the cause as based on the argumentation therein contained. There is no such title as this in the Decretals, but a sufficient understanding of its scope can be gained from a comparison of the *Corpus Iuris Civilis* (Roman law) and the few references to it in the *Corpus Iuris Canonici.* The actual trial, then, and the procedure even to its completion constitute the *litis instantia.*[1]

Article 1. The Position of the Litis Instantia in Judicial Procedure

In every judicial process there can be distinguished three major phases, namely, the introduction (*principium*), the body (*medium*), and the conclusion (*finis*). As Reiffenstuel (1642-1703) remarked,[2] the introduction can be said to extend from the presentation of the bill of complaint (*libellus*) or at least from the summons (*citatio*) issued to the adverse parties even to the joinder of issue (*litis contestatio*) inclusive. The *litis contestatio* is the cornerstone of the whole process. The body of the trial extends from the joinder of issue to and including the closing of the cause (*in causa conclusio*), and the conclusion (*finis*) of the whole process

[1] Reiffenstuel, *Ius Canonicum Universum* (5 vols. in 7, Parisiis, 1864-1870), Lib. II, tit. 1, n. 13.

[2] *Op. cit.*, Lib. II, tit. 1, nn. 1-3.

takes place with the rendering of the decision (*sententia*) and its execution.[3]

A clear concept of the nature and rôle of the *litis instantia* in relation to the major sections of the whole judiciary process was of obvious importance to the decretalists. Loose terminology in reference to the *iudicium, processus, causa* and *lis,* served to obscure that precision so necessary for a proper understanding of court procedure. How, then, were the *instantia, iudicium, processus, causa* and *lis* interrelated?

The *litis instantia* begins from the joinder of issue and normally closes with the passing of the sentence. Hence, the *instantia* is concerned with the body and the conclusion of the judicial process. Since it begins from the joinder of issue, the instance can be distinguished from the judicial process itself, which commences with the bill of complaint or at least with the summons served to the litigant parties.[4] Since the *iudicium* was often regarded as embracing the whole of the discussion of the cause from its introduction (*principium*) even to its conclusion (*finis*), it was sometimes also referred to as the judiciary process (*processus iudiciarius*), although Reiffenstuel said that its inception properly coincided with the joinder of issue.[5]

Where, then, did the *instantia* and *iudicium* differ? Briefly, it may be said that the concept of the *iudicium* includes at least three persons, the judge, the plaintiff, and the defendant, whereas the *instantia* refers directly to the plaintiff and the defendant only.[6] Reiffenstuel stated, however, that although the *iudicium* properly

[3] Reiffenstuel, *Op. cit., loc. cit.*

[4] Pirhing, *Ius Canonicum in V Libros Decretalium* (Dilingae, 1722), Lib. II, tit. 2, *De foro competenti,* n. 212 (hereafter cited *Ius Canonicum*); Reiffenstuel, *Ius Canonicum Universum,* Lib. II, tit. 1, n. 7.

[5] "Omissa litis contestatione, processus judiciarius est ipso iure nullus. Hinc ante litem contestatam proprie non dicitur judicium . . . . Et ea quae procedunt lite non contestata, proprie non dicuntur acta judicii sed praeparatoria ejus." — *Ius Canonicum Universum,* Lib. II, tit. 1, n. 18; cf. Bouix, *Tractatus de Judiciis Ecclesiasticis* (3. ed., 2 vols. in 1, Parisiis: apud Jacobum Lécoffre et Socios, 1885), p. 189.

[6] Reiffenstuel, *Ius Canonicum Universum,* Lib. II, tit. 1, n. 7; Santi, *Praelectiones Iuris Canonici* (4. ed., 5 vols. in 2, Ratisbonae, 1903-1905), Lib. II, tit. 1, n. 3.

begins from the joinder of issue, nevertheless, as to certain effects, it could also be said to begin with the summons (*citatio*).[7] Hence, it is evident that Reiffenstuel considered the *iudicium* a term which could be applied to both the *instantia* and the *processus iudiciarius*. The difference between the *processus iudiciarius* and the *instantia* consisted in that the former included the latter.[8] Not to be confused with the proper notion of the *instantia* is the judicial petition itself, sometimes called the instance, requesting the court to consider some aspect in the cause. Moreover, it should be observed that when the *instantia* is qualified by a numeral adjective, e.g., first instance, second instance, the word is used in designation of the jurisdictional stage in which the issue is being tried, e.g., court of second instance, i.e., the court of appeal.

The *lis* (controversy) is in a broad sense a more general term. In the *Lex Properandum* of Justinian[9] it was used as synonymous with *instantia*. It has also been used at times to signify the *causa*, that is, any dispute brought before a tribunal without relation to any particular phase of the judicial process.[10] Strictly taken, however, the *lis* or controversy is established only with the joinder of issue (*litis contestatio*), whereas the *causa* refers to the judiciary process without regard to the joinder of issue.[11] Finally, the *quaestio* or object of difficulty is differentiated from the *causa* in that it is a potential juridical issue not yet submitted to a tribunal of justice.[12]

[7] "Judicium incipit ab utroque sed diversimode. Nam a litis contestatione ita incipit judicium quod partes litigantes obligentur instantiae, simulque amplius non possint regulariter judicem recusare, sed teneantur coram eo, ubi lis contestata fuit, judicium finire. E contra, per citationem ita incipit judicium ut tamen reus necdum obligetur instantiae, imo possit libere, etiam actore invito, ab eo desistere, atque insuper ex justa causa adhuc possit recusare talem judicem et coram alio litigare."—*Ius Canonicum Universum*, Lib. II, tit. 1, n. 25.

[8] *Op. cit*, Lib. II, tit. 1, n. 26: "Unde sequitur quod instantia proprie incipit a litis contestatione, processus judiciarius vero a citatione."

[9] *C.* (3, 1) 13: "Ne lites fiant immortales . . . ."—*Corpus Iuris Civilis* (ed. P. Krueger et al., 3 vols., Berolini: apud Weidmannos, 1928-1929); Scott, *The Civil Law* (17 vols., Cincinnati: Central Trust Company, 1932), Vol. XII, *The Code*, pp. 260-263.

[10] Reiffenstuel, *Ius Canonicum Universum*, Lib. II, tit. 1, nn. 12-15.

[11] Reiffenstuel, *loc. cit.*; Pirhing, *loc. cit.*

[12] *Loc. cit.*

The foregoing distinctions should not be regarded as vain or specious in a study of this kind. Precision as to the exact meaning demands a thorough knowledge which can unravel the subtle or shaded differences which do exist in trial jurisprudence. They also demonstrate the fact that often in the past as in the present much of the terminology was used indiscriminately or at best synonymously.[13]

Article 2. The Acta Processus and the Acta Causae

Of grave importance also to the understanding of the *litis instantia* and the various limitations which may halt it is the distinction between the acts of the process (*acta processus*) and the acts of the cause itself (*acta causae*). Such acts as govern the order and formalities of a trial, e.g., the bill of complaint (*libellus*), the joinder of issue (*litis contestatio*), etc., insuring the orderly functioning of the procedure are called the *acta processus* in contradistinction to those acts, e.g., decisions, proofs, etc., which relate to the merits of the case, called the *acta causae*.[14] In the abatement of a trial (*peremptio instantiae*), in its renunciation, and when a subsequent trial follows, this distinction imports a very practical significance. Witness the effect caused by the *peremptio* of the instance. With the abatement of the instance the procedural acts (*acta processus*) lose their legal significance, but not so the *acta causae*. These latter maintain their value even in another trial,

[13] Witness the discrepancy of modern authors among themselves and from the above: "Contentio . . . cum vel sine respectu ad iudicium (sive in iudicium deducatur sive non) dicitur lis vel controversia, post litis contestationem proprie vocatur causa"—Beste, *Introductio in Codicem* (editio tertia, Collegeville, Minnesota: Saint John's Abbey Press, 1946), p. 775, footnote 12; "Cause . . . problème soumis au juge; ce mot est donc synonyme d'instance."—*Dictionnaire de Droit Canonique* (5 vols. and 3 fascicles [incomplete], Paris; Létouzey et Ané, 1924—) V, 1439-1440 (hereafter cited *Dictionnaire*).

[14] Reiffenstuel, *Ius Canonicum Universum*, Lib. II, tit. 1, n. 185; Lega, *Praelectiones inTextum Iuris Canonici* de *Iudiciis Ecclesiasticis*, (4 vols, Romae, 1896-1901), I, n. 385 (hereafter cited as *Praelectiones*); Wernz-Vidal, *Ius Canonicum* (7 tomes in 8 vols., Tom. VI, *De Processibus*, 2 ed., Romae: apud Aedes Universitatis Gregorianae, 1949), VI. 374 (hereafter cited as *De Processibus*).

and are worthy of judicial credence so long as the subsequent trial is the concern of the same litigant parties over the same issue in dispute.[15]

Under the law of the Decretals the *acta causae* were ruled to be of valid application only to those litigants who participated in the defense of their rights. In other words, the weight of proofs and decisions arrived at in the first trial were not to be made to burden in the second trial a person who had not previously had the opportunity to defend himself, i.e., who had not been a legitimate party to the first trial. Otherwise, a defenseless person, one who had not been heard, would be oppressed. Justice would be thwarted.[16] The *Regulae Iuris* of Boniface VIII put it succinctly: "Non debet aliquis alterius odio praegravari," and again, "Sine culpa, nisi subsit causa, non est aliquis puniendus."[17] Thus, all such matters as pertained to the merit of the cause were to be the concern of the litigant parties alone. To them alone should the benefit or the detriment therefrom accrue.[18] The commentaries of the later decretalists on this matter were wont to add a further condition to the value of the *acta causae* in subsequent trials, which condition was the proviso that a different mode of procedure be not employed in subsequent trials.[19] The reference was to subsequent ordinary trials as opposed to summary causes. The reason for this exception lay in the fact that summary trials did not employ such safeguards and formalities as did the ordinary trials. Ordinary trials were, therefore, more capable of forestalling fraud and error.

[15] *Decretales D. Gregorii Papae IX, una cum Glossis Restitutae,* (Romae, 1582), c. 11, X, *De testibus et attestationibus,* II, 20; *Corpus Iuris Canonici* (2 vols., ed. Lipsiensis Secunda, post A. Richteri curas . . . instruxit ab A. Friedberg, 2 vols., Lipsiae, 1879-1881), c. 11, X, *De Testibus et attestationibus,* II, 20.

[16] C. 2, *De sententia et re iudicata,* II, 11, in Clem.; C. 1, X, *De caus. poss. et propriet.,* II, 12.

[17] Regulae 22, 23, *R. J.* in VI°.

[18] C. 17, 25, X, *De sententia et re iudicata,* II, 27: "Res inter alios acta non noceat regulariter aliis juxta constitutiones canonicas et civiles." Cf. also C. 6, X, *De fide instrumentorum,* II, 22.

[19] Reiffenstuel, *Ius Canonicum Universum,* Lib. II, tit. 1, n. 181: "Sic enim acta probatoria seu attestationes receptatae in judicio summario fidem non facit in judicio ordinario . . . ."

Article 3. The Peremptio Instantiae and the Praescriptio Actionis

The length of time allowed by law to a right of action and the continued duration for the juridical exercise of that right of action must not be confused. The former has reference to the extinguishment of actions (*praescriptio*), the latter, to the abatement (*peremptio*) of the instance. It is most important to distinguish between how long a right of action lasts and how long the action itself is allowed to continue. In the former description we have the proper matter for *praescriptio,* in the latter, for *peremptio. Praescriptio,* then, extinguishes the right of action in a cause, whereas *peremptio* cancels the procedural acts of a cause. Both are affected by the element of time, *praescriptio* as to the time limit within which action must be brought, *peremptio* as to the time limit within which such action must be finished. Thus, the *instantia* can be distinguished from the *actio* as the exercise of a right of action in the judicial process is distinguished from the right of action itself.[20] Good faith is not a requisite for the abatement of the instance, whereas it is of necessity for the prescription of the right to an action in ecclesiastical law.[21]

A careful scrutiny of the distinction between the *acta causae* and the *acta processus,* and between the *peremptio instantiae* and the *praescriptio actionis,* thus solidifies that understanding of the decretal law which enables a keener penetration of the ramifications of this same matter in the Canon law of today.

[20] Cf. Lega, *Praelectiones,* I, n. 309.

[21] Reg. 2, *R. J.* in VI°: "Possessor malae fidei ullo tempore non praescribit." Cf. also Cc. 5, 8, 17-20, X, *De praescriptionibus,* II, 26; Wernz, *Ius Decretalium* (6 vols., Prati, 1914), V, n. 172, 7°; Schmalzgrueber, *Ius Ecclesiasticum Universum* (5 vols. in 12, Romae, 1843-1845), Lib. II, tit. 26, n. 116.

CHAPTER II

THE PEREMPTIO INSTANTIAE: ROMAN AND ECCLESIASTICAL LAW TO THE COUNCIL OF TRENT

Introduction

It is with the abatement of the *instantia* that the interest of this treatise in its historical conspectus is especially concerned. Without doubt, the *peremptio instantiae* is the most important institute one must study in order to obtain a greater depth of understanding not only of the institute itself but of the *litis instantiae* as a whole. Other elements of importance regarding the instance of a lawsuit one may profitably explore, but the accent of thought and research in this historical survey will rest on this major point.

The *peremptio instantiae* occurs when the judicial acts in a cause cease in such a manner that they can no longer allow of restoration. These procedural acts, as it were, die. The issue of the cause remains unresolved and a new process must be begun if the cause is to continue. The importance of the *peremptio instantiae* is evident to all who are involved in the legal procedure of the ecclesiastical courts. It has been deemed fitting, then, that the historical precedents of the *peremptio instantiae* be studied with a view to the better understanding of the present law[1] as gathered from its development in the past. This historical survey will extend to the establishment, modifications, restorations, and revisions of the law of *peremptio* as seen from the early days of the classical Roman period even to our time.

[1] *Codex Iuris Canonici, Pii X Pontificis Maximi iussu digestus, Benedicti Papae XV auctoritate promulgatus* (Romae: Typis Polyglottis Vaticanis, 1917, Reimpressio, 1933), Canons 1732-1741 inclusive.

Section I. Roman Law and the Peremptio Instantiae

Article 1. Some Basic Notions of Roman Procedural Law

To grasp the significance of the abatement or discharge of a lawsuit in Roman legal procedure it is necessary to understand beforehand some rudimentary notions of the Roman law of procedure itself. The history of a people's law begins with the history of the people itself, and in the grand system of law developed by the Romans there appeared three distinct phases, which reflected the nature of Roman society as it underwent changes through those early ages. Three systems of procedure appeared in succession: the first, the *legis actio* (so called to distinguish it from the formulary system in later days) was the outcome of an oligarchic system; the second, the *formula,* was created by a self-governing people; the third, the *cognitio,* was the outcome of autocratic bureaucracy.[2] Although among these systems there existed a kind of overlapping in the course of time, it has been claimed that the *legis actio* prevailed until the passing of the *lex Aebutia,* perhaps in the latter part of the second century B.C.[3] The formulary system was used chiefly from the last century of the republic until the end of the classical period (about 235 A. D., the death of Alexander Severus), and the *cognitio* (or *cognitio extraordinaria,* so called to distingush it from the *ordo* of procedure in the other two systems) was the system in use in post-classical times,[4]

The handling of a judicial action under the *legis actio* procedure, and later under the formulary system, was characterized by the division of the proceedings into two stages. The first stage of the procedure, which took place before the magistrate, was called

[2] Buckland, *The Main Institutions of Roman Private Law* (Cambridge: University Press, 1931), p. 345 (hereafter cited as *Main Institutions*).

[3] Jolowicz, *Historical Introduction to the Study of Roman Law* (2. ed., Cambridge: University Press, 1952), p. 179 (hereafter cited as *Historical Introduction*).

[4] *Loc. cit.*

in iure proceedings, and in it the magistrate supervised the arrangement of all the preliminaries to the trial. The second stage was said to be *apud iudicem,* i. e., before a judge who was neither a magistrate nor a professional lawyer, but who was appointed by agreement between the parties. It seems that the essential difference between the two systems in this twofold manner of procedure lay in differences of formality. Gaius (2nd century, A.D.) said that the result of the *lex Aebutia* and the *leges Iuliae* was to introduce litigation *per concepta verba,*[5] by words which could be adapted in each case to the particular matter in dispute, whereas the characteristic mark of the *legis actio* had been its use of unchangeable forms, *per certa verba.*[6]

In the formulary period the distinction between *in iure* and *apud iudicem* proceedings remained, but the joinder of issue, which fixed the subject-matter of the trial, was reached not in view of compliance with the forms of the *legis actio,* but in view of the formula set forth by the magistrate, which described briefly the point to be tried and the allegations of the litigant parties. This formulary system has been appropriately called the foundation of Roman law, because here is found the period where Roman substantive law was built up through the instrumentality of procedure.[7] The outstanding change in the *cognitio,* which superseded the formulary system in the third century, A. D., was the elimination of the traditional distinction between proceedings *in iure* and *apud iudicem.* This distinction disappeared entirely, so that the trial was conducted throughout by a state official.

Of particular importance in this study is a clear understanding of what constituted the *iudicia legitima* and the *iudicia imperio continentia.*[8] This distinction was perhaps due to the *lex Aebutia,*

[5] *Manuale delle Fonti del Diritto Romano,* Secunda Edizione per cura di Pietro Cogliolo (Torino: Unione Tipografico Editrice Turinense, 1911), pp. 354-355; Gaius (4,30).

[6] Jolowicz, *Historical Introduction,* p. 205; Leage, Roman Private Law (2. ed., reprint, edited by C. W. Ziegler, London: MacMillan and Co., 1951), p. 399.

[7] Leage, *Roman Private Law,* p. 404.

[8] Gaius (4, 103): "Omnia autem iudicia aut legitimo iure consistunt aut imperio continentur."

which extended the formulary system, and it enjoyed significance only under that system. Gaius said that the *iudicia legitima* were held between Roman citizens, before a single judge, and with the proceedings occurring within a mile of Rome itself.[9] All other proceedings belonged under the classification of *iudicia imperio continentia.* These latter depended on the praetor's *imperium* and were extinguished when it died. It is with this distinction between *iudicia legitima* and *iudicia imperio continentia* that the notion of *peremptio* comes into play. Inasmuch as the *imperium* of the magistrates in the provinces depended upon their yearly term of office, so it was that with the expiration of their term of office their power also expired. Cases begun and not completed within the term of office of such a magistrate were thus abated in the manner of an automatic discharge of the judicial process. For the sake of legality the procedure had to be reinstituted under the *imperium* of the new magistrate if the issue was to become adjudicated.[10] The action or right to pursue litigation upon the issue of the cause remained. The judicial process alone was affected.[11]

With the *iudicia legitima,* however, the judicial process remained indefinitely valid and thus was of legal effect until the final sentence of the cause was pronounced. It was due perhaps to the influence of the procedure of abatement in the *iudicia imperio continentia* that even the *iudicia legitima* later underwent a modification in so far as they, too, became subject to a similar limitation in time.[12] Thus the *iudicia legitima,* too, became subject to the limitations of *peremptio* with a time limit of eighteen months in which to conclude the proceedings. Some modern commentators claim that the *peremptio* in the *iudicia legitima* may have affected not only the

[9] Gaius (4, 104): ". . . inter omnes cives Romanos, sub uno iudice . . . quae in urbe Roma vel intra primum urbis Romae miliarium accipiuntur."

[10] Gaius (4, 105): ". . . . ideo autem imperio contineri iudicia dicuntur quae tamdiu valent quamdiu is qui ea praecepit imperium habebit."

[11] Jolowicz, *Historical Introduction,* p. 231, footnote 5.

[12] Gaius states: "Iudicia legitima . . . e lege Iulia iudiciaria nisi in anno et sex mensibus iudicata fuerint, expirant, et hoc est quod vulgo dicitur, e lege Iulia litem anno et sex mensibus mori." —Gaius (4, 104).

judicial process but also the right of action itself.[13] Were this true, the *peremptio* in the *iudicia legitima* would then also imply a *praescriptio* or statute of limitations upon the right of a plaintiff to bring action again. Another modern but opposite opinion maintains that, just as in the *iudicia imperio continentia,* so in the *iudicia legitima* the plaintiff retained his right of action notwithstanding the abatement of the judicial process.[14] Clarity in this matter is the reward of a further perusal of the remarks of Gaius. It is possible, from Gaius, to see why conflicting views regarding the plaintiff's right of action in the *iudicia legitima* exist among historians and commentators on Roman law.[15] Nevertheless, such conflicts can be resolved from these same remarks of Gaius. There is no difficulty with regard to the *iudicia imperio continentia.* In such causes the plaintiff did retain his right of action.[16] As to the *iudicia legitima,*[17] it seems that only actions *in personam* lost for the plaintiff his right for further action when the procedural acts exceeded the eighteen-month period set by law.[18] The fundamental point here to be made, however, is that it is in basic Roman law that the *peremptio instantiae* finds its root.

[13] Wernz-Vidal, *De Processibus,* p. 372; Lega-Bartoccetti, *Commentarius in Iudicia Ecclesiastica* (2. ed., 3 vols., Romae: Anonima Libraria Cattolica Italiana, 1950), II, 581, at footnote (hereafter cited as *Commentarius*).

[14] *Traité de Droit Canonique* (4 tomes, publié sous la direction de Raoul Naz, Paris: Létouzey et Ané; 1948-1949, IV, 220 (hereafter cited as *Traité de Droit Canonique*).

[15] "Iudicia legitima . . . nisi in anno et sex mensibus iudicata fuerint, expirant, et hoc est quod vulgo dicitur, e lege Iulia litem anno et sex mensibus mori." — Gaius (4, 104). The proponents of the loss of right of action in such causes evidently argue from the phrase *litem . . . mori.* But note the phrase . . . *hoc est quod vulgo dicitur.*

[16] "Et quidem imperio continenti iudicio actum fuerit sive in rem sive in personam . . . postea nihilominus ipso iure de eadem re agi potest . . ."—Gaius (4, 106).

[17] Cf. Adolph Berger, "Iudicia Legitima," *Encyclopedic Dictionary of Roman Law* (Philadelphia: The American Philosophical Society, 1953), p. 520.

[18] "Si vero legitimo iudicio in personam actum sit . . . postea ipso iure de eadem re agi non potest . . . si vero vel in rem vel in factum actum fuerit, ipso iure nihilominus postea agi potest . . . ."—Gaius (4, 107).

Article 2. Revision under the Autocratic Empire

The long centuries of the Roman empire, which developed after the metamorphosis of Roman society from its original oligarchic system and then its self-governing form, are generally divided into two periods. The earlier period, begun in the reign of Caesar Augustus (30 B.C. - A.D. 14) at the start of the Christian era and known as the Principate, saw the power of the emperor disguised under republican forms. This disguise, however, was wearing thin and vanished altogether in the third century A.D. The succeeding period of open autocracy is known as the Dominate era, since the emperor was then openly the master and not just the first citizen of the state. In 284 Diocletian ascended the imperial throne, and with his advent historians generally mark the dividing line between the aforementioned periods of the Roman empire.[19]

At the beginning of the Dominate period the formulary system was already obsolete, both in the provinces and in Rome itself. Even under the former system some causes had been adjudicated by the magistrate himself. Such causes, e. g., the *restitutio in integrum,* were the exception to the traditional *ordo iudiciorum.* The new system began to spread in the empire and under the Dominate period reached its zenith. The *cognitio* of this later Roman law was a procedural system in which the court proceedings were not based on the consent of the litigating parties, but it was the court itself which issued the summons to the defendant at the plaintiff's request. The whole case was tried by one magistrate from beginning to end. There were no two stages in the proceedings and the whole process was called *iudicium.*[20] Litigation now became an act of administration. The court was no longer merely a court of justice; it was a branch of a great bureaucratic system. Thus, with the abolition of the formulary system of procedure, and with the passing of the distinction between *iudicia imperio continentia* and *iudicia legitima* (all were now *iudicia imperio continentia*) the time length of the procedural acts in a cause was protracted indefinitely. They had become *perpetua.*

[19] Jolowicz, *Historical Introduction,* p. 3.
[20] Buckland, *Main Institutions,* pp. 386-388.

During this period a new type of jurisdiction, that of the ecclesiastical courts, acquired recognition. Even before Christianity had become the religion of the empire, Christians had been wont to bring their disputes before the bishop of their church or before his delegate.[21] The decisions of the bishops in such causes became binding also in civil law under Constantine (circa 312 A.D.), the first Christian emperor. Constantine allowed a litigant to bring his cause before a bishop for a decision, although proceedings had already been begun before a civil court, and this even against the wish of the other litigant.[22] The bishop was thus competent for all civil matters as well as ecclesiastical, and his judgment could be executed like those of the secular courts.[23]

The new Roman law of procedure underwent changes itself, however, for later emperors legislated freely on procedure. Under Constantine (307-337) it was not quite what it became under Theodosius II (438).[24] It has been noted[25] that the Council of Chalcedon (451) adopted some of these procedural modifications, particularly in cases of disputes among clerics involving ecclesiastical property. A revision of the legal structure of society, however, was much desired at this time. With the advent of Justinian and his legal advisers this hope was fulfilled.

Article 3. Restoration under Justinian (527-565)

The project of restating and reforming the law must have been in Justinian's mind even before he ascended the throne, for work

[21] I Cor., 6, 1-8.

[22] *Theodosiani Libri XVI, cum Constitutionibus Sirmondianis*, edd. Mommsen et Meyer, adsumpto apparatu a Krueger, 3 vols. (Berolini, 1905), *Const. Sirm. I; The Theodosian Code and Novels and the Sirmondian Constitutions* (a translation by Clyde Pharr, Princeton University Press, 1952), *I Sirmondian Constitution* (hereafter cited as *Theodosian Code*).

[23] Jolowicz, *Historical Introduction*, p. 469: Left to a later article will be the fuller discussion of the significance of this phenomenon and of its far-reaching importance.

[24] Buckland, *Main Institutions*, p. 336.

[25] Wernz, *Ius Decretalium*, V, n. 172.

upon it was begun almost immediately after he became emperor, and his codification was already completed in 534. This codification comprised the *Institutes,* the *Digest,* and the *Code,* which, together with the *Novels* or *Constitutions* enacted after 534 make up the *Corpus Iuris Civilis,* as the whole of Justinian's legislation has been called since the sixteenth century.[26] It is, however, to the study of the *peremptio instantiae* also that Justinian's law makes a striking contribution. It can safely be said that, since the early days of the Dominate empire, nothing really substantial was effected for a change of the perpetual nature of procedural acts in litigation. With Justinian, however, this state of affairs was seen as a public harm. Thus, in 530 he promulgated the Constitution *Properandum* in which, lest litigation become unending and be protracted beyond a man's life-span,[27] he declared that the judicial process in all contentious causes must be completed within three years from the commencement of the proceedings.[28] Criminal causes, he refers to, as already having been set for completion within a two-year limit.[29] There is some question, however, whether a *peremptio* of the judicial process was meant to occur automatically with the passing of the time limits, or whether Justinian meant to compel the judges to quicker action. From a reading of the law it seems that a duty was imposed upon the judges and that it was only through time and usage that practice made the operation of a *peremptio* automatic.[30] There are modern commentators on the history of law who, although conceding a possible difference of interpretation in the reading of the *lex Properandum,* assert strongly that a law of *peremptio* did not strictly exist under Justinian. It is

[26] Jolowicz, *Historical Introduction,* p. 485.

[27] ". . . ne lites fiant paene immortales et vitae hominum modum excedant . . ." —C. (3, 1) 13, *De Iudiciis.*

[28] ". . . non ultra triennii metas post litem contestatam esse protrahendas . . ." —C. (3, 1) 13.

[29] *Loc. cit.* : ". . . cum criminales quidem causas iam nostra lex biennio conclusit . . ."

[30] C. (3, 1) 13, 1: ". . . omnes iudices, sive in hac alma urbe sive in provinciis maiorem seu minorem peragunt administrationem, sive in magistratibus positi sunt vel ex aula nostra dati vel a nostris proceribus delegati, non esse eis concedendum ulterius lites quam triennii spatio extendere . . . ."

their contention that a *peremptio* properly so called had to become effective *ipso iure* with the passing of time in a way similar to the automatic operation which exists under the laws of the statute of limitation, whereas under Justinian, so they say, the law did not in itself intend to establish an automatic operation which the judges would merely apply, but rather it was a law directed at the judges to compel them to hasten court proceedings.[31]

It may be said at this point that one can hardly expect the historical antecedents of a law to be so exact in their composition as to coincide with the modern counterpart. All that can be expected in the historical study of an institute is that there exists a substantial semblance in the relevant matter. Needless to state, the contention of this study is that the *lex Properandum* of Justinian formed a major bulwark and base for the law of *peremptio* as we have it today.

There is no question, however, as to the universal scope of Justinian's law. The text itself makes this abundantly clear.[32] The only exception for lengthier terms of procedure was allowed in fiscal matters and affairs governing public functions.[33]

Justinian not only established the substance of the law on the *peremptio,* but ruled also as to the manner of making its operation effective. When the plaintiff through dilatory tactics impeded the continuance of the process to the point that the time limit was close at hand, the judge was to send agents six months prior to the procedural deadline, if necessary at three different intervals, in search of the plaintiff. If this venture proved unsuccessful, then with the expiration of the time limit the judge was to decide the cause from the evidence at hand and, if it was warranted, to exonerate the defendant completely, with the court costs being charged to the

[31] Wernz-Vidal, *De Processibus,* p. 372; Lega-Bartoccetti, *Commentarius,* II, 580.

[32] C. (3, 1) 13: "Properandum nobis visum est . . . praesentem legem super his orbi terrarum ponendam, nullis locorum vel temporum angustiis coarctandum ponere."

[33] C. (3, 1) 13, 1: ". . . exceptis tantummodo causis quae ad ius fiscale pertinent vel quae ad publicas respiciant functiones . . ."

estate of the delinquent plaintiff. If the evidence militated too conclusively against the defendant, then the sentence was in justice to show favor to the delinquent plaintiff, but the plaintiff was nevertheless to remain liable for the court costs. If the plaintiff complained later that the decision of the court did not go far enough in his favor, he was without the benefit of further action at court. The issue could not be resurrected, and the decision of the court remained final as a penalty for the plaintiff's delinquency.[34] If it was the defendant who was delinquent, the procedure was similar in its trend.[35] When, because of the death of the judge or for other unavoidable obstacles to the process of the cause, the set period of time limitation apparently could not be observed, the succeeding judge (whom circumstances might demand) was nevertheless to conclude the proceedings if there remained at least one year in which to do so. If less time remained, then the time limit for the proceedings was to be extended, so that the new judge would have one full year in which to complete the handling of the cause.[36]

The *lex Properandum* of Justinian served as a lubricant to the efficient operation of court proceedings. It will be seen that its influence was to carry not only into the glorious era of Canon law in the thirteenth century, but, after a setback, was to be revived so as to influence the ecclesiastical law of our own day.

[34] C. (3, 1) 13, 2c: ". . . actor contumax cadat omnimodo lite, si reus absolvetur; sin vero aliqua condemnatio contra reum pro absente actore proferatur, quam forsitan non sufficientem sibi actor putaverit fugitivus, nullo modo iterum eandem litem resuscitare concedimus. Et haec quidem poena actori fiat imposita. . . ."

[35] C. (3, 1) 13, 3: "Sin autem reus afuerit et similis eius processerit requisitio, quemadmodum pro persona actoris ediximus, etiam absente eo eremodicium contrahatur et iudex, secundum quod veteribus legibus cautum est, ex una parte cum omni subtilitate causam requirat et, si obnoxius fuerit inventus, et contra absentem promere condemnationem non cesset, quae ad effectum perducatur."

[36] C. (3, 1) 13, 8a: ". . . si quidem ex triennio annale tempus vel amplius residet, in quo alius iudex causae imponitur, intra reliquum tempus causa finiatur; sin autem minus quam annale sit, tunc omne quod deest repleatur. . . ."

Section II. Influence of Roman Law in Ecclesiastical Procedure

Article 1. Pre- and Post-Justinian Era to the Decretals

It was in the fourth century by the Edict of Milan (313) that the Church was freed from persecution and emerged from the catacombs with a status recognized by the civil government. For the first time the Church had the opportunity to develop its own judicial procedure and to regulate those causes which rightfully fell within the scope of its competence. Already from the beginning the Church had claimed the power to look into and settle disputes among its subjects.[37] Constantine favored the Church under his reign. It will be recalled that under Constantine the *audientia episcopalis* obtained concurrent jurisdiction with the secular courts. Under the Emperors Arcadius (398) and Valentinian III (452), however, the mutual consent of the litigant parties was prescribed for entering the episcopal tribunal.[38] There are also various other documents which reveal the exercise of this judicial power and the beginning of a form of judicial procedure in the Church.[39]

It is universally recognized that the procedural regulations of Roman law influenced the formation and development of canonical procedure.[40] That Roman law was a supplementary source for the ecclesiastical law is evidenced by Pope Saint Gregory I (590-604), who ordered that the rules of Roman law procedure be fol-

[37] I Cor., 5, 1-5; I Cor., 6, 1-8.

[38] Muirhead, *Historical Introduction to the Private Law of Rome* (2. edition revised by H. Goudy, 1899; 3. edition revised by A. Grant, London: A. and C. Black Ltd., 1916), pp. 343-347; Hogan, *Judicial Advocates and Procurators,* The Catholic University of America Canon Law Studies, No. 133 (Washington, D.C.: The Catholic University of America Press, 1941), p. 19; Clune, *The Judicial Interrogation of the Parties,* The Catholic University of America Canon Law Studies, No. 269 (Washington, D.C.: The Catholic University of America Press, 1948), p. 10.

[39] Tertullian, *Apologeticum,* cap. 39 — Migne, *Patrologiae Cursus Completus, Series Latina* (221 vols., Parisiis, 1844-1864), I, col. 460 (hereafter cited as *MPL*); Ottaviani, *Institutiones Iuris Publici Ecclesiastici,* I, 275.

[40] Schmalzgrueber, *Ius Ecclesiasticum Universum,* Lib. II, tit. 1, n. 4.

lowed in those points which were not regulated by ecclesiastical law.[41] Although this seems to be the first official recognition of Roman law as a subsidiary source for canonical procedure, it merely confirmed a current practice of the ecclesiastical courts. It is undeniable, then, that a deep influence was exercised upon the procedural laws of the Church, and this becomes even more evident from the study of the legislation as codified by Justinian.[42]

After the Germanic invasions in the fifth, sixth, and seventh centuries, there was left only a limited knowledge of Roman law in the West. The *Digest* had been forgotten and only abstracts of the Justinian *Code* and *Novels* were known, and most of these only in the form given by the Visigoths in the *Lex Romana.*[43] Little is known as to how the *peremptio* of Justinian's day fared in these times. Theoretically, it seems to have retained its official force, but the chaos and vicissitudes of the times certainly reduced its practical worth at least in the West.

About the year 1070 Justinian's *Digest* was rediscovered in a manuscript at Pisa. Its importance was quickly perceived by Irnerius (c. 1050-1130), a teacher at the University of Bologna, who began to expound it to his classes. This new impetus given to the study of Roman law was most opportune in the history of ecclesiastical judicial procedure. The renaissance of Roman law, a most momentous event in the history of the medieval world, was soon enhanced by Gratian with his counterpart study of Canon Law.[44] Thus, in the eleventh century, with the rediscovery of Justinian's work and the freeing of the ecclesiastical courts from secular con-

[41] *MPL*, LXXVII, 1294-1300.

[42] Benedetto Ojetti, "Ecclesiastical Courts," *The Catholic Encyclopedia* (15 vols., Index and 2 Supplements (New York, 1907-1922), IV, 453; Król, *The Defendant in Contentious Trials,* The Catholic University of America Canon Law Studies, No. 146 (Washington, D. C.: The Catholic University of America Press, 1942), p. 26.

[43] Haenel, *Lex Romana Visigothorum* (Berolini, 1849), p. 6; Laurin, *Introductio in Corpus Iuris Canonici* (Friburgi, Brisgoviae et Vindobonae, 1889), p. 266; Lane, *Matrimonial Procedure in the Ordinary Courts of Second Instance,* The Catholic University of America Canon Law Studies, No. 253 (Washington, D. C.: The Catholic University of America Press, 1947), p. 16.

[44] Kuttner, "The Father of the Science of Canon Law" — *The Jurist* (Washington, D. C.: The Catholic University of America, 1941), I (1941), 12.

trol (which subjection had come about in the centuries subsequent to the Germanic invasions), there began a new period in the development of the procedural law of the Church. The era of the *Decretum Gratiani,* the Decretals of Gregory IX, the *Liber Sextus* of Boniface VIII, the *Clementinae* of Clement V, the *Extravagantes* of John XXII and the *Extravagantes Communes,* all of which together were later to be known as the *Corpus Iuris Canonici,* was now to ripen into fruit.

Article 2. Modification and Change under the Decretals

A. The *Venerabilis Frater* of Honorius III

It can be said that as a whole the ecclesiastical courts adopted as sufficiently adequate the procedural laws of Justinian. The golden age of the Church had dawned, however, and with it more and more the development of Church law was perfected. With this systemization and growth, modifications were bound to be introduced. Such was the case with regard to the procedural norms of the *instantiae peremptio.* As a result of the growing practice on the part of litigant parties to use dilatory tactics, artificial obstacles, and even fraud in order to secure the abatement of lawsuits, ecclesiastical court procedure tended to become interminable and ineffective. To counteract this state of affairs Pope Honorius III (1216-1227) ruled that procedural acts could be continued to the completion of the cause notwithstanding the traditional three-year limit for abatement.

> "Venerabilis frater noster archiepiscopus Ravenas (Ravenna) proposuit coram nobis, quod, cum decisio causae . . . sit per subterfugia et cavillationes . . . per triennium prorogata, dicti Cervienses asserentes, instantiam iudicii per decursum triennii periisse, respondere . . . recusaverunt. Mandamus, quatenus, exceptione huiusmodi non obstante, in negotio isto procedas iuxta traditam tibi formam. . . ."[46]

The cause in question involved a jurisdictional dispute between the archbishop of Ravenna and a small neighboring community,

[46] C. 20, X, *de iudiciis,* II, 1.

which had by delays of one kind or another succeeded in preventing the completion of the lawsuit within the requisite three-year period. Pleading abatement of these proceedings on the grounds of the traditional Justinian time limit, the defending community refused to continue to participate in further hearings of the same instance. The archbishop of Ravenna thereupon had recourse to Rome, and Honorius replied with his historic decree.[46]

The interpretation of the decretals has been much aided by means of glosses which were added to the Decretal collections by a group of men nowadays referred to as the glossators. Their additions consisted of marginal notes, which had for their purpose the offering of a fuller explanation, the tracing of the sources, the deduction of certain conclusions, and the proposing of contrary or parallel texts.[47] It is through these glosses and glossators that one sees clearly into the memorable decree of Honorius. It appears that certain commentators of the time did not view the decree as necessarily voiding the *lex Properandum* of Justinian. They argued that the *lex Properandum* was not to be applied to the cause in hand. Further, they argued that although the instance of the lawsuit would otherwise be normally abated or perempted, the jurisdiction of the judge involved did not thereby come to an end. Hence, the judge would still be competent in the case. Moreover, unless the joinder of issue (*litis contestatio*) in the proceedings had been reached, there could be no question of the abatement of proceedings, since the *peremptio* applied only to proceedings after the joinder of issue. For the cause in point it was argued that there was no evidence of such a joinder of issue. By such reasoning these commentators sought to reconcile the decision of Honorius III with the *Properandum* of Justinian.[48] Another argument suggested that the *Venerabilis Frater* meant only to refer to judicial

[46] "Casus" — *Glossa Ordinaria* ad c. 20, X, *de iudiciis*, II, 1.

[47] Van Hove, *Commentarium Lovaniense in Codicem Iuris Canonici*, I, *Prolegomena ad Codicem Iuris Canonici* (second edition, Mechliniae et Romae: H. Dessain, 1945), p. 426.

[48] *Glossa*, s. v. *non obstante*, ad c. 20, X, *de iudiciis*, II, 1: ". . . Sed ex hac decretali non videtur quod lex illa, *Properandum*, corrigatur quia non collegitur hic quod lis fuit contestata sed per subterfugia et cavillationes causa sit prorogata, et hic potuit esse ante litem contestatam. . . ."

causes wherein subterfuge and dilatory tactics had been employed, that no divergence of procedure from the parallel civil law practice should be allowed without an express ecclesiastical law to that effect, and that the *Venerabilis Frater* of Honorius III did not constitute such an opposite law.[49] Rebuttal to this reasoning is found under the same gloss.[50] It was pointed out that the argument which was based on the absence of the *litis contestatio* was groundless inasmuch as from the very reading of the decretal it was evident that the joinder of issue had not only been reached in this dispute but had progressed even to the point where the attempt was made to prorogue the decision in the cause.[51] It was evident, then, that some modification had occurred. Pope Honorius, following the tradition of ecclesiastical procedure, necessarily saw the concept of the *peremptio* as based on Roman law. Nevertheless, the circumstances of his time and the demands of equity were enough to influence him to modify the *peremptio* as theretofore held under Justinian into what he (Honorius) considered a less rigorous mode.

B. Further Commentary and Reflections on the *Venerabilis Frater* vis-à-vis the law of *Peremptio*

The influence of Roman procedural law in the abatement of lawsuits continued to exercise its sway on the civil courts, notwithstanding the modification it had been seen to suffer in the ecclesiastical courts.[52] Then, too, the force of the *Venerabilis Frater* was debated even in ecclesiastical circles. Witness the argument as recorded by Panormitanus (1386-1453) when he discussed the force of the word *mandamus* in the decretal of Honorius III.[53] The point was, so Panormitanus contended, that Honorius did not

[49] Cf. Schmalzgrueber, *Ius Ecclesiasticum Universum*, Lib. II, tit. 1, n. 82.

[50] *Loc. cit.*

[51] *Ibid.*: ". . . lis contestata fuit, quia decisio etiam causae prorogata fuit . . . et sic fuit litis contestatio . . . et ex eo quod dicit instantiam iudicii periisse apparet quod processum erat in principali negotio, quod dicitur fieri per litis contestationem quae est principium causae. . . . ."

[52] Reiffenstuel, *Ius Canonicum Universum*, Lib. II, tit. 1, n. 31.

[53] Abbas Panormitanus (Nicholaus de Tudeschis), *Commentaria in Quinque Libros Decretalium* (5 vols., Venetiis, 1588), ad c. 20, X, *de iudiciis*, II, 1 (hereafter cited as *Commentaria*): "'Statuimus', illud verbum relatum ab habente potestatem legis condendae, inducit ius novum; secus verbum 'mandamus'."

make a new law as such, thus automatically abrogating the force of Justinian's *Properandum,* but rather proposed a solution to be followed in the particular cause in question, notwithstanding the regulation of the *Properandum* upon the *peremptio* of the judicial process.[54]

Nevertheless, the degree of the modification as found in the decretal proved too strong. Its effect was to change Justinian's law on this point. In practice, the civil law on the *peremptio* was not accepted in the ecclesiastical forum. Dilatory tactics and fraud thus served as an occasion for the further development of the equitable requirements of procedure. With growing frequency ecclesiastical judges had been unable to adjudicate the causes before them within the three-year time span. Thus, the seeming rigor of the *Properandum* and of the civil law procedure in this matter was discarded. In the ecclesiastical courts of first instance the lawsuit became again a procedure of indefinite time limit. When the cause had been appealed, however, and had evolved into its second instance, the Decretals prescribed that this second instance be concluded within a year or, at most, within a two-year period from the lodging of the appeal.[55]

With the common opinion of canonical commentators teaching that the *lex Properandum* no longer applied to ecclesiastical law, once again, as in the past, the danger of indefinite and unwieldy court procedure became imminent. No precise ecclesiastical law establishing a new norm for the abatement of lawsuits was made. To provide for this obvious defect, Canon law sought refuge only in indirect means (which were not conducive to efficiency) by instituting remedies against contumacious litigants. The *peremptio*

[54] ". . . nec Papa hic dicit quod instantia non perit, sed quod teneatur respondere, non obstante illa exceptione. Et pro hoc qua cum Papa non utatur hic verbo 'statuimus', nec alio verbo inducente ius novum, sed verbo 'mandamus', apparet quod non inducat ius novum. . . ."—*Loc. cit.*

[55] C. 5, X, *de appellationibus, recusationibus, et relationibus,* II, 28: "Appellans ad prosequendum habet annum et ex causa biennium, nisi iudex moderetur. Et si infra id tempus non prosequitur, rata manet sententia, vel redit ad primum si ante sententiam appellavit. . . ."; see also cc. 3, 6, 7, *de appellationibus,* II, 12, in Clem.; "Et qualiter finiatur"—Henricus de Segusio (Cardinalis Hostiensis), *Summa Aurea* (Venetiis, 1570), ad c. 20, X, *de iudiciis,* II, 1.

of court procedure was thus abandoned. The instance of a lawsuit had become relatively perpetual. Only the *praescriptio* of thirty years, the statute of limitation abolishing further right of action, could serve also in this indirect fashion and without practical value as the *peremptio* or abatement of court proceedings.[56] This state of the matter was to remain such until the sixteenth century and the Council of Trent.

Section III. The Peremptio Instantiae: The Development of the Ecclesiastical Law from the Council of Trent to the Code

Article 1. The Ruling of the Council of Trent

The Council of Trent (1545-1563) admittedly forms a milestone in the history of ecclesiastical law. Its canons and decrees on the many theological and disciplinary problems of the time have been much publicized. Because of the wealth of material with which it dealt, some of its decisions were of necessity overshadowed by others. Nevertheless, the Council of Trent did find time to treat of the problems created by excessively prolonged trials, and upon this matter it pronounced a rule and mode of action.

The old law of Justinian,[57] which had limited the *instantia litis* in contentious causes to a period of three years, had been itself modified by Pope Honorius III in 1220 for the ecclesiastical courts. With the passing of time the *instantia* again became *per se perpetua.* Many delays and much waste of time cluttered up the ecclesiastical courts. In its 24th reform session, in the twentieth chapter, the Council of Trent sought to remedy this state of affairs.[58] It appeared that the Council of Trent was reinstituting

[56] Reiffenstuel, *Ius Canonicum Universum,* Lib. II, tit. 1, n. 32; Schmalzgrueber, *Ius Ecclesiasticum Universum,* Lib. II, tit. 1, n. 82.

[57] *Lex Properandum,* C. (3, 1) 13.

[58] *Canones et Decreta Sacrosancti et Oecumenici Concilii Tridentini* (Parisiis, 1754) sess. 24, *de ref., c. 20——;* Schroeder, *Canons and Decrees of the Council of Trent* (St. Louis: B. Herder Co., 1941), pp. 211-213 (hereafter cited as *Council of Trent*): The decree in point stated: "Causae omnes ad *forum ecclesiasticum* quomodolibet pertinentes, etiamsi beneficiales sint, in prima instantia coram Ordinariis locorum dumtaxat cognoscantur, atque omnino saltem infra biennium a die motae litis terminentur. . . ."—Schroeder, *Council of Trent,* p. 479.

with modifications the ancient institute of a *peremptio instantiae.* Causes in their first instance were to be completed within two years after the joinder of issue.[59] This was the general norm thenceforth to be followed save for the exception of such causes as would be treated by the Holy See or in a special manner committed to other tribunals by the Holy Father.[60] Causes when appealed, e.g., to a court of second instance, continued in line with the norm established for them in Decretal law. The second instance was to be concluded within a year from the lodging of the appeal, and at any rate within two years when a serious reason intervened to postulate such a further grant of time.[61]

Difficulty in regard to meaning and interpretation came to attach itself to the following statement of the Council: ". . . alioquin post id spatium liberum sit partibus vel alteri illarum iudices superiores, alias tamen competentes, adire, qui causam in eo statu, quo fuerit, assumant et quam primum terminari curent. . . ."[62] From a reading of the law it seems that, if the aforementioned time limit was not observed, the litigant or litigants could approach competent judges of a superior tribunal to reach a conclusion for the cause at issue.

Article 2. Diversity of Interpretation

Since the time of Honorius III the jurisprudence of ecclesiastical courts had in practice maintained the perpetuity of the *litis instantia.* Giraldi (1692-1775) asserted that this practice was abrogated

[59] Giraldi, *Expositio Iuris Pontificii* (2. vols., Romae: ex Typographia Caroli Barbillini, 1769), I, Section 223 (hereafter cited as *Expositio*); Reiffenstuel, *Ius Canonicum Universum*, II, *Adnotatio* XXII.

[60] Giraldi, *Expositio, loc. cit.*: "Ab his excipiantur causae quae juxta canonicas sanctiones apud Sedem Apostolicam sunt tractandae, vel quas ex urgenti rationabilique causa judicaverit Summus Romanus Pontifex per speciale rescriptum e signatura Sanctitatis Suae manu propria subscribendum, committere aut avocare. . . ."

[61] C. 5, X, *de appellationibus, recusationibus et relationibus,* II, 28; Wernz, *Ius Decretalium*, V, n. 577; Cf. Lega, *Praelectiones*, I. n. 315.

[62] Schroeder, *Council of Trent, loc. cit.*

by the Council of Trent.[63] Referring to the Constitutions *Ad Romani* (July 10, 1574) and *Litium* (February 9, 1593) of Gregory XIII and Clement VIII respectively, Giraldi concluded that the ruling of the Council of Trent was confirmed by these popes later as applicable to the ecclesiastical courts in accord with the practice of the *peremptio instantiae* as it obtained in the secular courts since the time of Justinian.[64] Nevertheless, it was admitted by this same canonist that, notwithstanding the ruling of the Council of Trent, procedural practice had acted to weaken this ruling and conversely had established the perpetuity of the *instantia*.[65] The more common interpretation followed the opposite opinion, i. e., that the Council of Trent had not reinstituted an automatic abatement of the proceedings.[66] After the middle of the eighteenth century, however, the perpetuity of the existence of the *litis instantia* was admitted by all. The point of contention, having become academic, lay in the original interpretation of the Tridentine ruling. Much stress was placed upon the words: ". . . post id spatium liberum sit partibus . . . judices superiores adire. . . ."[67] In favor of the argument for the perpetuity of the instance was the fact that no contrary remedy had been established by the Council of Trent to thwart the longevity of the procedure. It provided only for a transfer of the cause to another tribunal.[68] It seems, then, that this latter interpretation was the correct one, since the transferred instance could simply be continued to its completion before the superior tribunal. It remained essentially the same *litis instantia*,

[63] "In hac decretali ('Venerabilis frater') statuit Honorius instantiam judicii non perire per lapsum triennium. Verum huic sanctioni derogatum est a concilio Tridentino, sess. 24, cap. XX, de reform. . . . . Quae conciliaris sanctio declarata est a Gregorio XIII et respective ampliata a Clemente VIII. . . ."—*Expositio, loc. cit.*

[64] *Expositio*, II, Section CLI.

[65] *Ibid.*, Section CCXXIII; Reiffenstuel, *Ius Canonicum Universum*, II, Adnotatio XXII.

[66] Barbosa, *Collectanea Doctorum tam Veterum quam Recentiorum in Ius Pontificium Universum* (Lugduni, 1656), in Cap. "Venerabilis", XX, *De foro competenti*, II, 1, Summarium, nn. 1-6.

[67] Schroeder, *Council of Trent*, pp. 211-213 and 479.

[68] Schmalzgrueber, *Ius Ecclesiasticum Universum*, Lib. II, tit. I, n. 82; Reiffenstuel, *Ius Canonicum Universum*, II, Adnotatio XXII, *in fine*.

i.e., the first instance, and was not to be considered as a matter of appeal. Wernz (1842-1914) aptly summed up the problem by remarking that this interpretation was more in conformity with the words of the Council of Trent and was well substantiated by procedural practice; itself the best interpreter of law.[69]

Article 3. Praxis Processualis

Whatever may have been the dispute over the interpretation of the ruling of the Council of Trent, the Sacred Roman Rota established its own solution. In a decision on litigation involving benefices (March 3, 1732) it ruled for the perpetuity of the *litis instantia*: " . . . de iure canonico instantia est perpetua."[70] Giraldi and Reiffenstuel cited a further Rota decision (March 28, 1757) to the same effect.[71] Although the *instantia* was now definitely termed *perpetua*, this was to be understood not in an absolute but rather in a relative sense, since a continued legal prescription of thirty years for judicial actions automatically and necessarily extinguished the lawsuit.[72] Ecclesiastical courts had adopted this thirty-year statute of limitation from the Theodosian Code at the time of the Council of Chalcedon (451). This statute of limitation had remained substantially unaltered throughout the succeeding centuries.

Through custom and by procedural practice there had already evolved two other ways by which the *litis instantia* could be abated. Even before the confirmative decision of the Rota on March 3, 1732, litigant parties could have taken practical advantage of the common interpretation in their favor, but it had not been their

[69] *Ius Decretalium*, V, n. 172: "Quae interpretatio uti verbis Concilii Tridentini est conformior, ita praxi quoque, quae optima est legum interpres, omnino confirmabatur."

[70] *Decisiones Sacrae Rotae Romanae coram R. P. D. Marcello Crescentio* (5 tomes, Romae: ex Typographia Joannes Zempel, 1754), II, *Tuden, Brochialis S. Christinae De Valeixe*, 3 martii, 1732, Summarium, nn. 4-6.

[71] *Decisio Sacrae Rotae Romanae in Barchinon. Jurisdictionis super Attentatis*, 28 martii, 1757, *coram Bussio*—Giraldi, *Expositio*, I, Section CCXXIII; Reiffenstuel, *Ius Canonicum Universum*, II, Adnotatio XXII (The original source could not be obtained).

[72] Wernz, *Ius Decretalium*, V, n. 172, footnote 117.

wont to do so in view of the expense involved. If there occurred a judicial declaration to the effect that the cause had been abandoned (which declaration could result in consequence of the fraud and deceit of the plaintiff or if ten years had elapsed from the introduction of the cause before the tribunal and simultaneously it was evident that the cause for the plaintiff was weak in its claims, then the *instantia* would be discharged.[73] Under such circumstances the delinquent party became liable for the court costs. Rotal decisions on March 21, 1727, and on January 23, 1730, confirmed this practice.[74] Thus, there developed two new modes in consequence of which there could result an abatement of the procedure, or a *peremptio*.

Except for the incidental influence of the institute of the *interruptio instantiae,* developed in later days, the law of the Church on the *peremptio* of the *litis instantia* as it then stood, continued unchanged, so that it remained applicable even to the advent of the Code of Canon Law in 1918.[75]

Article 4. Significance

Roman law and pre-Code Canon law based their application of the *peremptio instantiae* upon such motives as the demand of the common good and the need of fit punishment for negligent litigant parties. Unwieldy and prolonged court proceedings were a detriment to equitable efficiency within the juridic structure of society.

A cursory but significant glance at the history of this institute clearly establishes the fact that, except for unsubstantial alterations, Roman law as stated by Gaius (middle 2nd cent.)[76] excercised its influence throughout the subsequent centuries. Emperor

[73] Giraldi, *Expositio,* 1, Section CCXVIII; Reiffenstuel, *Ius Canonicum Universum,* Lib. II, tit. I, nn. 29-30; Schmalzgrueber, *Ius Ecclesiasticum Universum,* Lib. II, tit. 1, nn. 79-80.

[74] *Decisiones Rotales in Ferrarien. Capellaniae,* 21 martii, 1727, Quoad vero *coram Crispolto et in Pampelon, Beneficii de Villa Franca,* 23 ianuarii, 1730, 'Quam cum ita se habent' *coram Cencio*—Giraldi, *loc. cit.* and Reiffenstuel, *loc. cit.* (Original sources could not be obtained).

[75] Wernz, *Ius Decretalium,* V, nn. 572-577; Santi, *Praelectiones Iuris Canonici,* Lib. II, tit. 1, n. 6.

[76] *Gaius* (4, 103-107).

Justinian (527-565) rejuvenated the institute[77] and by the force of his monumental Code firmly fixed it in the jurisprudence of the Roman world and of Christendom. The Church adopted the *peremptio* from Justinian's law. In the thirteenth century there did come a rejection of it, but only in the ecclesiastical courts. The civil law was to retain it even to our own day. Moreover, the ecclesiastical courts meant not to supplant, but only to modify it. It was practice and interpretation that caused the rejection of the *peremptio instantiae*.

With the Council of Trent a restoration of this institute was attempted. Once again, a variance of interpretation along with a variant procedural practice of the ecclesiastical courts rendered it ineffectual. In recompense, the same jurisprudence which had seemed to repudiate the *peremptio* nevertheless resurrected it, although under less rigorous modes. The codification of Canon Law was to complete the historical cycle by reverting substantially to the basic concept of the institute, thus halting the vicissitudes which the *peremptio instantiae* had witnessed in the course of the centuries.[78]

[77] *Lex Properandum*, C. (3, 1) 13.
[78] Canons 1736-1739.

CHAPTER III

THE RENUNCIATION AND THE INTERRUPTION OF THE INSTANTIA

Section I. The Renunciation of the Instance

Article 1. Notion and Indications in Ancient Law

The renunciation of the instance of a lawsuit is fundamentally a simple concept. It had and has a close affinity to the notion of the *peremptio instantiae.* The same general effects occurred as in the *peremptio* with the exception that the party who made the renunciation paid the expenses of the court.[1] The renunciation of the instance consisted in the waiver of the lawsuit by either or both of the litigant parties in such a way that the procedural acts thus far established were set aside without, however, a relinquishing of the right to bring action again.[2] The renunciation of the instance has also been spoken of, though improperly, as a mode by which the *peremptio instantiae* was effected. When so regarded, the notion of the renunciation received treatment in connection with the consideration of the effects of the abatement or *peremptio* of the instance, since the effects of both the *peremptio* and the renunciation (with the exception of the added burden of court expenses, as noted above) were the same.[3] The *peremptio instantiae,* however, involved an automatic abatement of the procedural acts, whereas the *renuntiatio instantiae* gave rise to a voluntary abatement. The renunciation of the prosecution was not to be confused, moreover, with the reunciation of the right to an action at law, nor, for that matter, with the renunciation of certain procedural acts. One could renounce the prosecution without thereby relinquishing the right

[1] Wernz, *Ius Decretalium,* V, n. 577.

[2] Lega, *Praelectiones,* I, n. 316.

[3] Lega, *Praelectiones,* I, n. 316, footnote 2.

to bring action again. One could, moreover, renounce some procedural acts of the instance without thereby renouncing the instance itself.[4]

The *renuntiatio instantiae* as such was unknown to early Roman law.[5] One could renounce a lawsuit by withdrawing the complaint before all further procedure. Under the law of the Twelve Tables a litigant could lose judgment in his favor by forfeiture, i. e., if he did not appear by midday on the appointed day for trial and had no legitimate excuse. In that event the judge was to give judgment for the party who was present.[6] Such procedure, however, had little which is comparable to the *renuntiatio instantiae* for, once the issue at point was decided by sentence, no further action could be brought; or, if the complaint had been withdrawn before the hearing took place, the matter had really never come to trial.

Under Justinian's law the parties could renounce the lawsuit, thus bringing the judicial proceedings to a final conclusion. This renunciation, however, meant that the right of action was renounced. Hence, the parties could not again restore action for the prosecution of their cause.[7] This was a far cry from the *renuntiatio instantiae* as such, in which the judicial proceedings were renounced without a simultaneous relinquishing of the right to bring future action on the same matter of dispute. Hence, whatever indications of the *renuntiatio instantiae* existed in Roman law, they bore little similarity to the institute which was to develop in later times.

It was primarily to the *peremptio instantiae* as used and influenced by forensic practice in canonical and civil procedure that the institute of the *renuntiatio instantiae* owed its origin and later development. In other words, the *renuntiatio instantiae* emerged

[4] *Codicis Iuris Canonici Fontes,* cura Emi Petri Card. Gasparri editi, 9 vols., VII-IX, editi cura et studio Emi Iustiniani Card. Serédi, (Romae [postea Civitate Vaticana]: Typis Polyglottis Vaticanis, 1923-1939), n. 6459, can 34, 1 (hereafter cited as *Fontes*).

[5] Lega, *Praelectiones,* I, n. 316, footnote 2.

[6] Jolowicz, *Historical Introduction,* p. 188.

[7] C. (2, 3) 4: "Postquam liti . . . motae renuntiasti, causam finitam instaurari posse nulla ratio permittit."

from the *peremptio instantiae,* but was shorn of its involuntary and automatic operation.[8] The important development of the renunciation of the instance, then, was to come later in history.

Article 2. Development

It belonged to the judiciary rules of Gregory XVI in 1834[9] and to the later *Lex Propria*[10] and the *Regulae Servandae*[11] at the Roman Rota, of 1908 and 1910 respectively, to establish firmly the procedure to be followed in the renunciation of the prosecution of an instance in the ecclesiastical courts.

Gregory XVI ruled that the renunciation had to be a pure and simple declaration in writing, not restricted by conditions or reservations. It was to be subscribed to by either the renouncing litigant or his procurator who, however, needed a special mandate so to act.[12] Moreover, the renunciation of the instance required the acceptance of it by the adverse party.[13]

Did this disposition of law mean that, without necessarily involving a renunciation of the whole instance, one or some of the procedural acts of the instance could be renounced? Gregory XVI, in the title of the section treating of renunciation,[14] spoke of the

[8] Cf. Lega, *op. cit., loc. cit.*

[9] *Regolamento Legislativo e Giudiziario per gli Affari Civili emanato dalla santità di Nostro Signore, Gregorio Papa XVI con Moto Proprio dal 10 novembre, 1834* (Roma: dalla Tipografia Camerale, 1834), Sezione VI, *Della rinunzia agli atti della lite* (hereafter cited as *Regolamento Legislativo*).

[10] *Acta Apostolicae Sedis, Commentarium Officiale* (Romae: Typis Polyglottis Vaticanis, 1909), II (1910), 346-347, num. 20 (hereafter cited as *AAS*); *Fontes* n. 6459: *Lex Propria S. R. Rotae et Signaturae Apostolicae,* 29 iun, 1908.

[11] *Fontes,* n. 6461, *Regulae Servandae in Iudiciis apud S. R. Rotae Tribunal,* 4 aug. 1910.

[12] *Regolamento Legislativo* § 912: "La parte che intende rinunziare agli atti della lite, ne farà la dichiarazione in cancellaria. Tale dichiarazione sarà pura e semplice, e senza condizioni o riserve; sarà sottoscritta dal rinunziante, o dal suo procuratore in virtù di speciale mandato."

[13] *Regolamento Legislativo,* § 915; cf. Tuschus, *Practicae Conclusiones Iuris in Omni Foro Frequentiores,* Tom. IV, ed. 3 (Lugduni, 1689), p. 306 at c. 216.

[14] "Sezione VI, *Della rinunzia agli atti della lite*" — *Regolamento Legislativo,* at the head of § 912.

renunciation of the acts of the process. From the contents of this whole section,[15] there is no specific reference to the renunciation of one or some procedural acts alone. It is the opinion of the present writer that, at least in so far as the language of the regulations of Gregory XVI was concerned, the rules on the renunciation — "*della rinunzia agli atti della lite*" — did not refer to one or some procedural acts, but dealt rather with the acts as a whole. Further confirmation of this view derives from the definite reference to all the procedural acts, hence, the instance as a whole, when the *Regolamento* stated: "La rinunzia fatta dall' attore o dal reo, dopo proferita la sentenza, equivale ad una cosa giudicata irretrattabile contro il rinunziante."[16] The renunciation, however, of one or only some of the acts after the sentence was passed would in no way have resulted in a *res iudicata* for the cause. Thus, it is inescapable to the writer that Gregory XVI was speaking of the procedural acts of the cause as a whole.[17] Be that as it may, the *Regulae Servandae* did indicate a solution of this question less than a century later.

According to Gregory's rules, two principal effects derived from the renunciation of the instance. If the renunciation was admitted by the judge and not impugned by the adverse party, then the matters renounced were to be considered as restored to the state in which they existed before judicial action was brought regarding them. Moreover, the one who made the renunciation was to recompense the other party for his expenses.[18]

The *Lex Propria* of the Roman Rota (1908) and the *Regulae Servandae* (1910) further clarified the whole matter. The codifi-

[15] *Regolamento Legislativo*, Sezione VI. § 912-915.

[16] Ibid., § 913.

[17] Cf. Wernz, *Ius Decretalium*, V, n. 172, footnote 113, and Lega, *Praelectiones*, I, n. 316, footnote 2, where the effects of the renunciation spoken of in the *Regolamento*, § 913 and 915 respectively, were treated in reference to the *renuntiatio instantiae;* cf. also Lega-Bartoccetti, *Commentarius*, II, 601, footnote 2.

[18] *Regolamento Legislativo*, § 915: "La rinunzia ammessa dai giudici, ovvero non impugnata dalla parte, produce in ogni caso i seguenti effetti; 1) che le cose s'intendano rimesse di pieno diritto nel medesimo stato in cui erano prima degli atti in essa compresi; 2) che il rinunziante, in virtù dell' atto di rinunzia, debba ritenersi come condannato a pagare le spese in favore dell' altra parte."

cation of the law of the Church was then already in progress, and there is no doubt that the rulings of 1908 and 1910 must have influenced the *renuntiatio instantiae* in modern ecclesiastical law. The *Lex Propria* of 1908 incorporated the rulings of Gregory XVI. It also served to make them more precise. The renunciation of some procedural acts as well as of the whole instance was considered. It clarified the manner of procedure to be followed in the renunciation. Such renunciation had to be accepted first by the adverse party or, at least, not opposed by him, and admitted by the judge.[19]

Two years (1910) later, the *Regulae Servandae* further elaborated the pronouncements of the *Lex Propria*. Thus, the renunciation could take place at any time during the judicial process.[20] The renunciation made after the *sententia,* however, had equivalently the effect of an irrevocable *res iudicata* in the cause on the side of the renouncing party.[21] The renunciation had either to be accepted by the adverse party or, at least, to be made known to him and to be unopposed by him.[22] Having adopted the same standard procedure which the *Lex Propria* of 1908 had incorporated and refined from the rules of Gregory XVI, the *Regulae Servandae* of 1910 went a step farther. In causes touching spiritual affairs and the public good, the presiding judge could overrule the objections made by the adverse party to the renunciation when such objections

[19] *Lex Propria,* can. 34, 1: "Si introducta causa, actor renunciare velit instantiae aut liti, aut causae actibus, id ei semper licebit. Sed renunciatio debet esse absoluta nullique conditioni subiecta, subsignata cum loco et die a renunciante, vel ab eius procuratore, speciali tamen mandato munito, ab altera parte acceptata aut saltem non oppugnata, et a iudice deinde admissa."

[20] *Regulae Servandae,* § 219, 1: "Pars quae ad normam can. 34 (*Lex Propria*) intendit renuntiationem emittere, id potest efficere in quocumque statu et gradu causae. . . ."

[21] *Ibid.,* § 220: "Renunciatio facta ab actore vel a reo post sententiae prolationem, aequivalet rei iudicatae irrevocabili contra renuntiantem." The term *res iudicata* implied that a cause was considered irrevocably adjudged, so that it could not be opened again by any court in ordinary procedure. Cf. Woywod-Smith, *A Practical Commentary on the Code of Canon Law* (revised edition, 2 vols., New York: J. F. Wagner, Inc., 1952), II, 341.

[22] *Ibid.,* § 219, 4: "Ut renuntiatio suum sortiatur effectum, acceptata sit oportet ab altera parte, cui facienda est notificatio; subintelligitur autem acceptata si, intra congruum temporis terminum a Ponente assignandum, non oppugnetur."

were out of order and without foundation.[23] Thus, the question of the acceptance of the *renuntiatio instantiae* or of some of its acts was resolved.

The *praxis processualis* of the Rota, as has been seen,[24] had served before to fix the law of procedure in matters of the *instantia*. Inasmuch as the Rota held the position of an ideal to the lower diocesan courts,[25] its practices obtained in those same courts. Hence, the development and growth of the *renuntiatio instantiae* can be profitably studied from the regulations and decisions followed by the Roman Rota.

Section II. The Interruption of the Instance

Article 1. Notion

The interruption of the *instantia* occurred when the procedural acts in the trial were halted in such a manner that the *instantia litis* could for a time be no farther evolved. In this limitation the interruption was similar to a suspension of the cause. There was, however, a notable difference between the two. A trial was said to be suspended when some event not affecting the juridical status of the litigant parties occurred to impede the trial's further progress, whereas it was interrupted when the juridical status of the parties or of their procurators was changed.[26] Hence, a suspended trial could be restored and continued apart from any necessary formalities. The interrupted trial, on the other hand, called for a formal method of procedure, since the legal status of either or both of the parties had been so affected that the right to stand in trial (*ius standi in iudicio*) was modified. The reassumption of an interrupted trial, however, did not introduce a new trial; it simply was the continuation of the same.

[23] *Ibid.*, § 219, 6: "Renuntiatio ab altera parte aut tempore debito non oppugnata, aut in causis spiritualibus et in aliis ad bonum publicum spectantibus, iis rationibus oppugnata, quae iudici videantur non attendendae, et hinc a iudice admissa sine acceptatione alterius partis, nihilo secius plenum sortitur effectum iuridicum."

[24] Cf. *supra*, pp. 26-27.

[25] Cf. Suarez, *Tractatus de Legibus et Legislatore Deo*, Vols. V-VI of the Opera *Omnia* (28 vols., Parisiis, 1856-1861), Lib. VII, c. 5, n. 15.

[26] Wernz, *Ius Decretalium*, V: p. 437, n. 572; *Dictionnaire*, V, 1440-1441.

Article 2. Roman Jurisprudence and Development in Canonical Procedure

The *interruptio instantiae* developed in canonical and civil jurisprudence. As in the institute of the *renuntiatio instantiae,* so at most only some indications of the *interruptio instantiae* existed in Roman law. The *translatio iudicii* of Roman law, however, was somewhat similar to it. The *translatio iudicii* was an alteration in the procedural formula in a specific trial after the issue was joined, i.e., after the *litis contestatio.* Such an alteration became necessary when there existed a change of the person involved in the trial.[27] In the event of a substitution made by the judge, or of a mutation of status in the litigant parties or of their procurators, Roman law allowed a transfer of the trial to another tribunal.[28] The technical side of the *translatio iudicii* was not quite clear. It is even possible that all occurrences of the *translatio iudicii* were not treated in the same way.[29] Moreover, the very nature of this *translatio iudicii* was disputed. Wenger (1874-1953) stated that the solution could perhaps be found in this, that the parties went through a second act similar to the *litis contestatio,* in the formula of which, however, it was expressed that not a new trial but rather a change in an already existing procedural relationship was involved.[30] The *translatio iudicii,* however, had no more than the relationship of similarity to the *interruptio instantiae* as later developed in the ecclesiastical courts.[31]

The transfer of the trial was not to be the major note in the development of the *interruptio instantiae.* The effect of the *ius standi in iudicio* determined its role in canonical procedure. The mutation of the status of a party could result in the loss of the right

[27] Adolph Berger, "Translatio iudicii" — *Encyclopedic Dictionary of Roman Law* (Philadelphia: The American Philosophical Society, 1953), p. 741.

[28] D. (5, 1) 60: "Mortuo iudice quod eum iudicare oportuerat, idem eum qui subditus est sequi oportet." Cf. D. (5, 1) 76, where it is stated that the process remains the same even though the judges have been changed, and also Wernz-Vidal, *De Processibus,* n. 412, footnote 6.

[29] "Translatio iudicii" — *Encyclopedic Dictionary of Roman Law,* p. 741.

[30] *Institutes of the Roman Law of Civil Procedure,* revised edition, translated from the German by O. H. Fisk (New York: Veritas Press, 1940), p. 184.

[31] Wernz-Vidal, *De Processibus,* n. 412, footnote 6.

of the party to stand in trial.[32] In Roman law the *capitis diminutio* was in its effects equivalent to the loss of the *ius standi in iudicio.* The *capitis diminutio* of Roman law was that loss of the civil status of a person which implied the legal inability to conclude valid transactions and to be the subject of rights as recognized by law. Hence, the person who had suffered the *capitis diminutio* was devoid of the right to bring procedural action as a citizen of the Roman state.[33] Since excommunication, insanity, etc., did in canonical procedure entail the loss of the *ius standi in iudicio,* and since these defects could occur while the proceedings were in progress, consequently the loss of the right to stand in trial could result in the interruption of the judicial process.[34]

Obviously, the *instantia* was interrupted by the death of one of the litigant parties: "Mors enim omnia solvit."[35] When the trial involved litigation over ecclesiastical benefices and either or both of the litigants had died, Decretal law had established whether the judicial proceedings could continue and how and to whom the benefice should be adjudged.[36] The defunct parties involved in these proceedings had, naturally, undergone a change in status. Pope Clement V decreed under which circumstances the litigation could continue. When both parties had died, the trial was not to proceed, since the matter then pertained to the Pope or to the ordinary for a final settlement; otherwise, the surviving litigant or a party in interest[37] could continue to prosecute the cause. This was an exception to the usual effect caused by a change of status, for, as it

[32] Devoti, *Iuris Canonici Universi Publici et Privati Libri Quinque,* 3 vols., Romae: (1837), Tom. III, *De Iudiciis,* XVII: "Sed nec omnes in iudicio stare permittuntur, et horum e numero sunt infantes, furiosi, amentes . . . . , pupilli sine auctoritate tutoris . . . minores annis 25 sine auctoritate curatoris . . . , excommunicatus vitandus. . . ."; Reiffenstuel, *Ius Canonicum Universum,* Lib. II, tit. 1, n. 149.

[33] "Capitis diminutio"—*Encyclopedic Dictionary of Roman Law,* pp. 380-381.

[34] Devoti, *op. cit., loc. cit.*

[35] Wernz, *Ius Decretalium,* V, n. 572 and n. 172, 1.

[36] C. 1, *ut lite pendente nihil innovetur,* II, 5, in Clem.

[37] "Si non prosequeretur, lis non penderet."—*Ibid., Glossa,* s. v. *Prosequatur.* If the interested party did not pursue the litigation, the instance did not remain pending. Whether the *peremptio* thus effected entailed the loss of the right to further action was not stated.

seems, the nature of the subject matter, involving the *bonum publicum* and the interest of the Church, demanded that litigation concerning the rights in respect to the holding and conferring of benefices should be determined. Much later in history it was clearly stated by Gregory XVI that, as long as the judicial deliberation in the cause had been concluded, the death of a litigant did not forestall the rendering of the decision.[38] In all this, however, the point to be considered is that death entailed a change of status, and hence an *interruptio instantiae* was effected.

The change of status, then, generally effected the interruption of the instance. Not every change, however, sufficed, but only such a juridical change in status which impeded one's right to stand in trial.[39] The concept of the juridical change in status of the litigant parties had also existed in Roman jurisprudence,[40] but, as it has been seen, the consequence of its effect generally was the *translatio iudicii.* That a juridical change in status could effect the *interruptio instantiae* in canonical procedure may also be inferred from the *Regolamento* of Gregory XVI. By law, the procurator undertook the rôle of the principal litigant when the principal party had died or had suffered a change in status.[41] When, however, the procurator who acted for his client ceased to exercise his office, this new change of status interrupted the continued prosecution of the cause.[42] In 1918 the newly codified law of the Church was to incorporate the substance of these rulings with reference to the *ius standi in iudicio* and to apply them to the *interruptio instantiae.*[43]

[38] *Regolamento Legislativo,* Sezione V, § 906: "La denuncia della morte o del seguito cambiamento non impedisce che la causa venga giudicata, quando ne sia comperita anteriormente la discussione, e non rimanga che la sola pronuncia della sentenza."

[39] Wernz, *Ius Decretalium,* V. n. 572 and n. 172.2.

[40] D. (5, 1) 4, where Gaius is quoted to the effect that one in subjection to another cannot be a party adverse to this other in a trial: "Lis nulla nobis esse potest cum eo quem in potestate habemus. . . ."

[41] *Regolamento Legislativo,* Sezione V, § 903: "Allorchè, in pendenza di una lite, abbia luogo la morte o il cambiamento di stato di una delle parti, la legge ritiene come padrone della medesima il di lei procuratore."

[42] *Ibid.,* § 909.

[43] Canons 1733-1735.

Article 3. Significance

The element common to the interruption, to the renunciation, and to the *peremptio* of the instance was the cessation of the proceedings in the actual prosecution of the trial. Each of them so affected the lawsuit as to halt its progress. They all contributed, in a close affinity, to an understanding regarding the rôle and importance of the *litis instantia*. This similarity ended, however, in their effects.

The *peremptio* caused the most drastic halt to the prosecution of the instance. It has been likened to an institute in the nature of a penalty.[44] At best, it always implied at least a tacit renunciation of the instance. The *renuntiatio instantiae,* on the other hand, although it resulted in the same practical effects, was less drastic in the mode of its procedure, since it was the express renunciation of the instance on a wholly voluntary basis. The *interruptio* was the least potent in this matter, since it did not cause the extinction of the instance. Whereas in the *peremptio* both parties shared in the expenses of the court, in the *renuntiatio* only he who initiated the renunciation was liable for the court costs and reimbursement to the other party. Of itself the *interruptio* had no bearing on this matter.

A precisely formulated concept of the *instantia litis* carries with it a clear understanding of the above-mentioned institutes. Only thus can the nature and rôle of the *instantia* be wholly intelligible. In the preceding pages the writer has therefore stressed these institutes in the belief that through such a historical study of the *litis instantia* there could be provided a solid background for a deeper insight into the rôle it plays in modern ecclesiastical law.

[44] *Dictionnaire,* V, 1444.

PART II

CANONICAL COMMENTARY

CHAPTER IV

GENERAL ASPECTS OF THE LITIS INSTANTIA

Article 1. The Notion of the Litis Instantia

The *litis instantia* is the actual argumentation in the trial. It begins with the joinder of issue and concludes with the passing of the judicial sentence.[1] The concept of the *litis instantia* as defined by the commentators of the pre-code law,[2] remains substantially the same and is basic in the Code of Canon Law.[3]

The distinctions and correlations made in the historical survey of this dissertation[4] concerning the various notions of judicial procedure, e.g., *iudicium, processus, instantia,* etc., are not only appropriate but decidedly helpful in this canonical commentary. Some further clarification, however, may be of benefit, since modern commentaries may at times speak of these various notions of judicial procedure in a sense somewhat alien to that contained in this study.

The Code defines the *iudicium ecclesiasticum* (the ecclesiastical trial) as the legal discussion and settlement before an ecclesiastical

[1] Canon 1732: Instantiae initium fit litis contestatione; finis autem omnibus modis, quibus iudicium terminatur, sed et antea non solum interrumpi, verum etiam finiri potest sive peremptione sive renuntiatione.

[2] Reiffenstuel, *Ius Canonicum Universum,* Lib. II, tit. I, n. 13: "... instantia est actualis excitatio iudicii incipiens a litis contestatione usque ad sententiam. . . ."

[3] Cf. canon 1732; Wernz-Vidal, *De Processibus,* p. 369, n. 409: "Instantia sumitur . . . pro actuali exercitatione seu exercitio actionis et complectitur omnes actus iudiciales ordinatos ad causam instruendam et definitiva sententia terminandam."; Coronata, *Institutiones Iuris Canonici* (3. ed., 5 vols., Taurini et Romae: Marietti, 1947-1951), III, p. 164, n. 1259 (hereafter cited *Institutiones*): "Litis instantia est exercitium actionis in uno eodemque gradu . . . ."; Lega-Bartoccetti, *Commentarius,* II, 565: "Instantia est exercitium actionis iudicialis." Cf. also Augustine, *A Commentary on the New Code of Canon Law* (8 vols., Vol. VII, 2. ed., Saint Louis: Herder and Co., 1925), VII, 180.

[4] Cf. *supra,* Part I, *Historical Conspectus,* pp. 2-4.

tribunal of a controversy in an affair over which the Church has the right to judge.[5] In Roman law the *iudicium* was that complexus of judicial acts performed by both the judge and the parties which enabled the resolving of the point in dispute.[6] Under Decretal law, a judicial process seemed to refer to the acts performed by the judge in the cause,[7] and hence constituted only a part of the *iudicium* as defined in Roman law. It is claimed that in modern ecclesiastical law, however, a judicial process (*processus iudiciarius*) refers to all those judicial acts by which the rights of litigant parties are safeguarded.[8] Under this aspect the judicial process as referring to all judicial acts has a wider range than the *iudicium* in modern ecclesiastical law, since the *iudicium* strictly begins with the joinder of issue.[9]

Sometimes a distinction is also drawn between the notion of a judicial process, as described above, and the procedure itself, inasmuch as the latter refers more to the external and practical development of the process.[10] In practice, however, the notions of *iudicium, processus iudiciarius,* and *procedura* (procedure) are often taken interchangeably to signify any of the foregoing concepts.[11] The same should not be done with the concept of the *litis*

[5] Canon 1552, § 1: Nomine iudicii ecclesiastici intelligitur controversiae in re de qua Ecclesia ius habet cognoscendi, coram tribunali ecclesiastico, legitima disceptatio et definitio. Cf. Woywod-Smith, *A Practical Commentary on the Code of Canon Law,* II, 223. Note that the execution of the sentence is not a necessary part of the essence of this definition.

[6] D. (2, 12) 6; Roberti, *De Processibus,* I, p. 55, n. 31.

[7] C. 5, X, *de feriis,* II, 9.

[8] Roberti, *De Processibus,* I, p. 56, n. 31.

[9] Cf. Vermeersch-Creusen, *Epitome Iuris Canonici* (3 vols., Vol. III, 6. ed., Mechliniae-Romae: H. Dessain, 1946), III, 1. The *iudicium,* which strictly taken begins with the joinder of issue, is, as it were, a part of the judicial process taken as a whole. Cf. Coronata, *Institutiones,* III, p. 164, n. 1259; Cf. also, however, Lega-Bartoccetti, *Commentarius,* I, 2, where to the contrary the understanding of the notion of *processus* seems to revert to that of the Decretals: ". . . notio processus quae se habet uti partem iudicii necessariam et comprehendit complexum legum quibus determinatur modus disceptandi causas easdemque definiendi apud iudicem."

[10] Roberti *loc. cit.*

[11] *Loc. cit.*

instantia. True, the judicial instance of the prosecution period of a trial is operative within the greater framework of the judicial process considered as a whole, but the prosecution is only a part of the judicial process. It is also true that the instance is co-extensive with the *iudicium* (taken in its strict sense), since both begin with the joinder of issue. The instance, however, refers directly to the plaintiff and the defendant, whereas the *iudicium* necessarily includes by direct reference the person of the judge.[12] In other words, the instance of the lawsuit is judicial because it is necessarily an important facet of the judicial process; primarily and in itself, it is the judicial contention between the litigant parties.

Roberti well explains the real distinction between the judicial process and the action itself, but in his explanation he seems to equate the notion of *processus* with that of *instantia.*[13] That there is a real distinction between the judicial process and the action[14] is readily admissible. An action denotes the potential prosecution of a right, whereas the process points to the means in and by which someone tests that action. The action (that right of seeking in a trial what is one's due) is founded in the law which concedes the right of prosecution. The process, however, is founded in that disposition of law by which the judge at the petition of the plaintiff, is bound to carry out the law.[15] For these reasons it is evident that the *actio* is distinct from the process itself.

[12] Lega-Bartoccetti, *Commentarius,* II, 565.

[13] Roberti, *De Processibus,* I, p. 61, n. 34: "Doctores minus recentes, quos quidam etiam ex recentioribus sequuntur, haud perfecte actionem a processu distinguunt. Communis fuit apud Canonistas definitio: 'instantia est exercitium actionis' seu 'actio in actu secundo'; in qua definitione processus praebetur veluti actio ipsa in sua actuatione." Note how Roberti identifies *processus* with *instantia.* Incidentally, against his argument one can reply that the test of an action by trial is distinct from the action itself. Hence, the *actio* and the *exercitium actionis* can still remain really distinct.

[14] *Actio* is the "ius persequendi in iudicio quod sibi debetur"—Lega-Bartoccetti, *Commentarius,* II, 565. This is derived from the definition "actio autem nihil aliud est quam ius persequendi iudicio quod sibi debetur", as furnished by Justinian in his *Institutes* (4, 6) proemium.

[15] Roberti, *De Processibus,* I, p. 61, n. 34.

What at first glance appears difficult to understand is why there is an equation of the judicial process with the *instantia* Are not the *introductio libelli* (introduction of the bill of complaint) and the *citatio* (summons) procedural acts, or, to be more exact and to avoid confusion of terminology, acts of the judicial process (*acta processus*)? Then, if this be so, it seems most unlikely that an equation between the notions of *processus* and *instantia* can exist, for the Code of Canon Law itself states in its very first canon on the *litis instantia* that the instance of the lawsuit begins with the joinder of issue.[16] Obviously, there can be no *litis contestatio* without the necessary prelude of something about which to contest, which preliminary is constituted through the bill of complaint, the summons to the parties involved, etc. Hence, one must conclude that, when Roberti states that the instance of the lawsuit is the same as the process,[17] he means to stress rather the second part of his statement, wherein he says that the *instantia* is a certain phase of the process.[18]

It will not be without profit, therefore, to enumerate at the outset of this canonical commentary the various shades of difference which exist among modern commentators in defining the *litis instantia.* It has already been remarked that the pre-Code terminology remains substantially the same today, although commentators vary somewhat in their explanations. Uncertainties in signification and inconsistencies of terminology combine to produce difficulties of understanding. For the purpose of clarification these shades of meaning should be made known. Hence, a preliminary clearing of possible confusion is in order.

Reiffenstuel (1642-1703) defined the *litis instantia* as the actual argumentation in the trial, beginning with the joinder of issue and concluding with the passing of sentence or with the passing of the three-year time limit for proceedings (*peremptio*).[19] In substantial

[16] Canon 1732: Instantiae initium fit litis contestatione. . . .

[17] "Instantia idem est ac processus . . ." — *De Processibus,* II, p. 3, n. 307.

[18] ". . . aut certa phasis eiusdem." — *Loc cit.*

[19] *Ius Canonicum Universum,* Lib. II, tit. 1, n. 13 ". . . instantia est actualis excitatio iudicii incipiens a litis contestatione usque ad sententiam vel saltem usque ad finem triennii."

agreement was Vidal (1867-1938) who defined the *instantia* as the implementation of the judicial action embracing all those judicial acts which look to the development of the controversy in litigation, and the termination thereof by a definitive sentence which becomes irrevocable (*res iudicata*).[20] Noval (1861-1938) reiterated the same thought with the express comment, if the writer understands him correctly, that by *sententia* he meant a firm decision (hence, a *res iudicata*), since the instance relates also to a tribunal of superior rank.[21] Coronata defines the *instantia* as the implementation of the judicial action in one and the same stage of the trial. From his explanation it is evident that he considers the close of the instance accomplished by way of a definitive sentence alone, i. e., through the settlement of the principal matter of litigation in the trial,[22] and not necessarily, therefore, by way of an irrevocable judgment. It has already been seen that Roberti defines the *instantia* as being the process itself or a certain phase of the process. Roberti strives to correct that definition of the *instantia* which calls it the *exercitium actionis*.[23] To him such a terminology involves a confusion of the *actio* with the *processus*.

From the foregoing explanations of what constitutes the *litis instantia* there can be deduced two major shades of difference among the commentators. First, is the *exercitium actionis* the correct expression of the essence of the *instantia?* Secondly, does the

[20] *De Processibus*, p. 369, n. 409: ". . . instantia sumitur . . . pro *exercitio actionis* et complectitur omnes actus iudiciales ordinatos ad causam instruendam et definitiva sententia terminandam. . . . *finis* instantiae fit omnibus modis quibus iudicium terminatur. Iudicium autem . . . terminatur modo ordinario per sententiam definitivam, quae in rem iudicatam transierit."

[21] *Commentarium Codicis Iuris Canonici*, Liber IV, *De Processibus*, Pars I, *De Iudiciis* (Romae: Marietti, 1920), p. 297: "Litis instantia est litis agitatio, seu actionis exercitium per actus iudiciales ordinatos ad causam probationibus instruendam et sententia definitiva ac firma terminandam. Dicitur 'firma' quia ad tribunal superioris gradus protenditur litis instantia." (hereafter cited *De Iudiciis*).

[22] *Institutiones*, III, p. 164, n. 1259: "Litis instantia est exercitium actionis in uno eodemque iudicii gradu . . . . Modus naturalis quo finitur iudicium et proinde etiam instantia litis est sententia definitiva, qua data appellari potest novam instantiam inchoando."

[23] *De Processibus*, II, p. 3, n. 307 and I, p. 61, n. 34.

instantia normally close with the definitive sentence in one and the same stage of the trial, i. e., with the passing of sentence in the court where the cause is first tried or does it extend also to another stage of the trial, i. e., to the court of appeal, and end only by the passing of an irrevocable judgment?

With regard to the first question there is no doubt that the *actio* is distinct from the *instantia,* as the right of seeking in trial what is one's due is really distinct from the medium in and by which that right is tested. Does, however, the expression *exercitium actionis* confuse this right to sue with the medium in which this right is tested? It appears not to do so. The right to do something and the actual doing of that something are metaphysically as really distinct as potency and act.[24] Concretely, the *exercitium actionis* should be understood to mean the actual progress by trial in the resolving of whether there is a legitimate foundation for the action which has been brought to litigation, i.e., whether that action is worthy of judicial protection. There should be noted the apparent difference of stress in the definition by Reiffenstuel, namely, *actualis excitatio iudicii,* from that of Noval, Vidal, and Coronata, namely, *exercitium actionis.* It is understandable why one could easily believe that some modern jurists confuse the *actio* with the *processus.* A comparison, however, should not be made between the *excitatio iudicii* and the *exercitium actionis.* Herein arises the confusion. Rather, it is *actualis excitatio* which should be compared to the *exercitium actionis.* It is the *actualis excitatio* iudicii, then, which should be equated to the *exercitium actionis* of the trial.

The possibility, however, that there may in fact exist a confusion in understanding the *actio* as not really distinct from the *instantia* should also not be overlooked. It appears to this writer that this possibility is realized in the second question or problem stated. In other words, there is an intimate relation of the first problem to the second. When Vidal and Noval spoke of the termination of the trial, and hence of the *instantia,* by way of an irrevocable decision (*res iudicata*), it appears that they confused

[24] This holds true for the very sound reason that they *are* metaphysically *potentia* and *actus.*

the *actio* with the *instantia*. Inasmuch as the action lasts until an irrevocable decision is reached,[25] perhaps it was thought that therefore the same instance continues notwithstanding the definitive sentence which is not a *res iudicata*. Since, however, the status of persons is never irrevocably adjudicated,[26] the opinion of Vidal and Noval should logically eliminate the *litis instantia* from such trials, e.g., in marriage causes. Obviously, such a conclusion cannot be maintained. Coronata, happily, does not reach the same conclusion. He clearly states that the normal way by which the trial and also the *instantia* ends is by way of a definitive sentence in the cause, which, if appealed, gives rise to a new instance.[27]

An interesting reflection is made by Lega-Bartoccetti when, after defining the *instantia* as the implementation of the judicial action, they state that the trial is not fully completed until the sentence in the cause becomes irrevocable. Hence, in a wide sense, a trial may include several instances, i.e., in the first, second, and further stages or steps of the trial. Lega-Bartoccetti observe, however, that the *litis instantia* does close with a definitive sentence by which the judge accomplishes his task. In one and the same trial, moreover, there can be several instances in so far as conjointly with the principal object of litigation there are decided several incidental questions.[28] It is the opinion of this writer that Coronata and Lega-Bartoccetti are correct on both of these questions of difference among modern commentators, although it is easily admitted that the term *exercitium actionis* can be misleading. On the first question, therefore, there is no confusion between the right to prosecute an action and the actual test of that action in trial. On the second question, canon 1732 expressly states that the *litis instantia* concludes by any of the ways in which the trial is concluded; an irrevocable judgment is not necessary, therefore, to conclude the *instantia*.

[25] Canon 1904, § 1: Res iudicata praesumptione iuris et de iure habetur vera et iusta nec impugnari directe potest.

Canon 1904, § 2: Facit ius inter partes et dat exceptionem ad impediendam novam eiusdem causae introductionem.

[26] Cf. canon 1903.

[27] *Institutiones*, III, p. 164, n. 1259.

[28] *Commentarius*, II, 565-566.

In summary, then, it may be said that the *litis instantia* in a wide sense is sometimes taken synonymously with *processus,* since the *instantia* does constitute a part of the judicial process. In its proper sense, however, the *litis instantia* is that phase of the judicial process which begins with the joinder of issue (*litis contestatio*) and comprises all those judicial acts, e.g., the judicial interrogation of the parties, the taking of proofs, etc., which look to the completion of that trial by way of a judicial sentence (*sententia*). The apparent difficulty with regard to the concepts inherent in the terminology is thus resolved. In its resolution the profit of a precise knowledge in the matter of this subject is attained.

Article 2. The Inception of the Litis Instantia

The *litis instantia* begins with the joinder of issue.[29] It is through the joinder of issue that the point of controversy between the litigant parties is precisely defined. The remainder of the judicial proceedings sees the controversy as defined in the *litis contestatio* developed by various proofs and finally resolved by means of a judicial decision (*sententia*). The joinder of issue (*litis contestatio*) consists in the formal denial by the defendant of the claim made by the plaintiff with the intention of litigating the case in court.[30] Although no solemn procedure as such is required for the joinder of issue, nevertheless the fact of the complaint by the plaintiff and the denial thereof by the defendant (all of which takes place before the judge), wherein the points of the controversy are determined, is inserted into the acts of the case and becomes part of the *acta processus*.[31]

The practical effects of the *litis contestatio* are enumerated in canon 1731. The bill of complaint becomes fixed, i.e., the plaintiff may not change the bill of complaint without the consent of the defendant and of the judge. The bill of complaint, however, is not considered changed when the manner of proof alone is altered, or when the claims are reduced. Nor is it considered substantially

[29] Canon 1732.

[30] Canon 1726: Obiectum seu materia iudicii constituitur ipsa litis contestatione, seu formali conventi contradictione petitioni actoris, facta animo litigandi coram iudice.

[31] Canon 1727.

changed when the facts alleged are further illustrated, completed, or amended, provided that the object of the controversy remains the same. Moreover, no substantial change of the original joinder of issue occurs if, instead of the object itself, the price of interest or something equivalent is substituted. The judge prescribes a sufficient period of time for the parties to propose and complete their proofs, although this period of time may be extended at the discretion of the judge. With the joinder of issue the possessor of the goods or rights in litigation ceases to possess in good faith.[32] Should the case be decided against him, the possessor must restore not only the object concerned but also any emoluments which may have accrued to the object since the issue was joined.[33]

The *litis instantia* is the natural sequel to the *litis contestatio.* In the mechanical aspects of judicial procedure it may even be regarded as the general effect of the *litis contestatio.* The commencement of the *litis instantia* takes place with the determination of the issue to be litigated. Until the object of the trial is established, there can be no real progress towards a judicial solution of a complaint placed before the court. With the determination of the issue, on the other hand, the judicial process can begin to move towards a solution. This is precisely where the *litis instantia* begins. The effect of the *litis contestatio* is to prevent a substantial alteration in the issue as joined. The litigant parties are now committed to the quarrel as submitted to the court. Hence, once the issue is joined, the instance of the lawsuit begins. Thus, the commencement of the *litis instantia* is contained implicitly among the effects of the *litis contestatio* as enumerated in canon 1731.[34]

[32] Woywod (*Practical Commentary,* II, 287) stated that the possessor is not thus constituted in bad faith. Since the goods or rights are now in litigation, he may be considered a possessor in doubtful faith. Vidal (*De Processibus,* p. 365, n. 405, note 22) called this cessation of good faith on the part of the possessor the *mala fides iuridica,* i. e., the positive law holds the possessor to be juridically without good faith, notwithstanding the subjective good faith of that possessor.

[33] Canon 1731, 3°

[34] Lega-Bartoccetti, *Commentarius,* II, 565: "Solet recenseri inter effectus contestationis litis per hanc scilicet haberi *instantiae initium.* Reapse hic habetur, uti statuit c. 1732. At hic effectus implicite contine[n]tur in tribus effectibus quos ponit c. 1731; quare in hoc tit. VIII dispicitur de instantia quae fluit a litis contestatione."

The question and objection may be proposed, however, that the *litis contestatio* is not strictly necessary for the judicial process. In treating of the contumacy of the defendant who refuses to answer the summons for the joinder of issue, canon 1844, § 2, rules that the decision (*sententia*) of the court in such an event should cover only the claims made in the bill of complaint.[85] Does this regulation obviate the necessity for the *litis contestatio?* The question should be answered in the negative. The fact of the matter is that, notwithstanding the usual procedure of joining the issue, *de facto* there does exist an equivalent *litis contestatio,* since the object or matter of the litigation does become determined. Obviously, some object for litigation must be had. In the event that the defendant is in contempt of the court by his refusal to appear, the original bill of complaint becomes the basis for the lawsuit.[86] Thus, the *litis instantia* begins when it becomes evident that the defendant will not appear for the normal procedure in joining the issue. With such contumacy in evidence, the original *libellus* becomes the basis for the lawsuit, thereby establishing the subject matter for the trial and thus there results an equivalent *litis contestatio.*

Article 3. The Termination of the Litis Instantia

The *litis instantia* ends in any of the ways in which a trial may be concluded.[87] There are many ways, some direct, some indirect, by which a trial may end. Normally, a definitive sentence closes the trial.[88] This is the natural and direct way by which a trial con-

[85] Si procedatur ad sententiam definitivam, lite non contestata, sententia respicere tantum debet petita in libello; si lite contestata, ipsum contestationis obiectum.

[86] Woywod-Smith, *Practical Commentary*, II, 323: "The plaintiff does not win his case by the very fact that the defendant refuses to appear, either at the beginning of the trial or at any later stage of the same: he must prove his claim and the judge must conscientiously examine the proofs. If no joining of issues took place through the contempt of court of the defendant, the original bill of complaint is the basis for the suit; the plaintiff has to prove what he claimed in his bill, and the judge passes sentence on the claim in the bill; if the joining of issues took place, those issues are the basis of the trial, and, after the plaintiff has proved the counts in the issue, the judge must pronounce sentence on the issue."

[87] Canon 1732: ". . . finis autem omnibus modis, quibus iudicium terminatur."

[88] Cf. canon 1868, § 1.

cludes. Of itself such a sentence settles the controversy that was litigated in court. As far as the nature of the cause permits, the definitive sentence determines what the losing party must give, do, or refrain from, how that obligation is to be fulfilled, and who is to defray the court costs. The definitive sentence must contain the reasons in fact and in law on which it is based.[39] Through the closing of the trial by way of the definitive sentence, then, the *litis instantia* itself is terminated.

The abatement of the instance (*peremptio instantiae*) and the renunciation of the instance (*renuntiatio instantiae*) are direct means also whereby the instance may be concluded. These means however, are abortive in their character, for they end the instance without allowing it to reach its goal, i.e., the sentence. Of these the succeeding chapters will treat in detail.

It may be asked: what of the decree executing the judgment? Does not the *litis instantia* also envisage it and therefore conclude with the execution of the sentence? It has already been seen that the judicial process is composed of a series of judicial acts undertaken in the treating and the expediting of matters of judicial import,[40] whereas the ecclesiastical trial (*iudicium*) is simply the legal discussion and settlement of a controversy over which the Church has a right to pass judgment.[41] It should be remembered, however, that *iudicium* (trial) and *processus* (judicial process) are in practice often taken interchangeably.[42] If, in reference to the problem posed above, one equates the *processus* with the *iudicium* (as in practice many do), then with the conclusion of the *iudicium* by way of a judicial sentence[43] the judicial process also must close. Thus the acts subsequent to the passing of the sentence would be extrajudicial. If, however, the *iudicium* is considered as part of

[39] Canon 1873.

[40] Cf. Coronata, *Institutiones*, III, p. 1, n. 1086.

[41] Canon 1553, § 1.

[42] Cf. Goyeneche, *De Processibus* (2 vols., pro manuscripto: Romae, 1948) I, p. 6, n. 2, who states that the term *processus* can have properly two acceptations: it may be considered in practice as the *iudicium*, or it may include also those acts which concretely safeguard the rights determined by means of a judicial sentence, hence, the execution of the judicial sentence.

[43] Cf. canon 1552, § 1.

the process then with the passing of the judicial sentence that part of the process, i. e., the *iudicium,* ends. Thus, it is not unlikely that the execution of the judicial sentence can be considered as a procedural act subsequent to the judicial sentence. If on the other hand, one considers the judicial process as part of the *iudicium,*[44] then one can argue for the administrative nature of the execution of the judicial judgment, since the judicial process will end with the close of the *iudicium* of which it is a part, by way of the judicial judgment. The importance of a discriminating juridical terminology is thus again made obvious.

The question, therefore, is: does the execution of the sentence constitute a part of the *litis instantia?* Roberti makes the observation that modern authors hold for the inclusion of the execution of judgment within the definition of ecclesiastical trial, dividing contentious trials into two stages, the discussion and settlement of the controversy, and the execution thereof.[45] Noval stated that the execution of the sentence is implicitly contained in the definition of an ecclesiastical trial, as given in canon 1552, § 1.[46] It may seem, therefore, that the execution of a sentence may also be contained, at least implicitly, in the *litis instantia.* It is admitted, however, that the second stage of this division of the trial, i.e., the execution of the sentence, is often lacking in merely declarative processes. Moreover, as far as the criminal trial is concerned, the execution of the sentence is considered to be an administrative act.[47]

From the foregoing it may be stated that when the Code does not distinguish then no distinction seems called for. Hence, when canon 1552, § 1, defines the ecclesiastical trial as the legitimate discussion and settlement (*legitima disceptatio et definitio*) of the controversy, it should be taken at face value. In this definition there is no mention made of the execution of the sentence.[48] Canon

[44] Cf. Lega-Bartoccetti, *Commentarius,* I, 2.

[45] *De Processibus,* I, p. 57, n. 32.

[46] *De Iudiciis,* pp. 5-6, nn. 16-17.

[47] Roberti, *De Processibus,* I, p. 57, n. 32.

[48] Indeed, this explanation is more consonant to the juridic tradition which has come down to us from the Middle Ages. Cf. Roberti, *De Processibus,* I, p. 57, n. 32.

1732 states that the *litis instantia* ends in any of the ways in which the *iudicium* terminates. The *iudicium* normally closes with the judicial sentence. Hence, the *litis instantia* terminates with the judicial sentence. In other words, the *litis instantia* does not include the execution of the judicial sentence.

A trial may also end indirectly, i.e., without attaining its natural goal, the sentence. It may at times happen that the plaintiff is in contempt of the court by failure to appear in obedience to a summons, whether this be at the beginning of the trial or during its progress. If at the first summons the plaintiff remains absent without sufficient or any excuse, the judge at the request of the defendant may issue a new summons. Should this second summons be not obeyed, then the judge at the request of the defendant (or of the promoter of justice or of the defender of the bond, if they are concerned) is to issue a declaration that the plaintiff is in contempt of the court.[49] The defendant can thereupon petition the court either to allow him to be discharged in the cause, or to be freed from the claim of the plaintiff, or to declare null and void all the acts thus far performed in the cause. Moreover, should he so prefer, the defendant may petition the court to continue the cause even in the absence of the plaintiff.[50] The effect of such contumacy on the part of the plaintiff is to deprive him of the right to continue the instance, i. e., to prosecute his cause further in this trial.[51] The party in contempt is bound to pay the court costs which result from his contumacy and to indemnify the other party when expenses and loss were caused to the other party through such contumacy.[52] Thus, the *litis instantia* may be terminated by the discharge of the lawsuit upon the contumacy of the plaintiff.[53]

Another way by which the *litis instantia* may terminate is the simple compromise (*transactio*). When a civil (contentious) controversy in private affairs has been submitted to the court for settlement and yet there appears to be some hope for friendly settle-

[49] Canon 1849.
[50] Canon 1850.
[51] Canon 1850, § 1.
[52] Canon 1851, § 1.
[53] Cf. Wernz-Vidal, *De Processibus*, p. 369, n. 409.

ment out of court, the judge should strive to get the litigant parties to compromise their differences, since it is highly desirable that litigation be avoided among the faithful.[54] The judge may seek this manner of settlement at any time that he deems it most opportune and effective, hence, even during the progress of the trial.[55] Unless the divine or ecclesiastical law be opposed, such a compromise should follow the rules of the civil law in the place where it is made.[56] Here is had an example of where the Code "canonizes" the prescriptions of the civil law. No compromise, however, can validly be effected in criminal causes. Nor can it be effected in causes pertaining to ecclesiastical benefices when there is litigation about the title to a benefice, nor in spiritual matters when the compromise would require payment for the spiritual goods in terms of material value. Moreover, the compromise as a means of settlement is excluded in causes wherein the marriage bond is involved.

The effect of the compromise is called *compositio* or *concordia,* i. e., a friendly settlement or agreement. The expenses incurred in the reaching of this settlement are equally shared by the litigant parties, unless a different arrangement has been reached between them, or unless the court has expressly ruled otherwise.[57] Thus, a trial already in progress may be abruptly halted by means of a compromise between the litigant parties. Accordingly, the *litis instantia* can terminate in this indirect manner.

The decisive oath (*iusiurandum decisorium*) is still another way by which the *litis instantia* may cease. The decisive oath is an oath taken as a means of settling the dispute in litigation. It may be taken by either party to the controversy, not only before the controversy has begun in court but also during the trial.[58] At any time or stage of the cause one party may with the approval of the judge ask this oath of the other party with the understanding that the controversy (whether it be the principal question in litigation or an incidental one) will be settled upon the taking of this oath.

[54] Canon 1925, §1.
[55] Canon 1925, § 2; Wernz-Vidal, *De Processibus, loc. cit.*
[56] Canon 1926.
[57] Cf. canon 1928.
[58] Canon 1834.

The decisive oath, however, can be asked only under certain conditions.[59] The party who has requested the decisive oath may recall his request before the oath is taken. The other party is free to accept the request and to take the oath, or he may refuse it, or reverse the request to the first party.[60] If the oath is accepted and taken, the matter in controversy is settled in the same way as though a compromise or settlement in court had been made.[61] If the request for the decisive oath is reversed by the party requested to the party making the request, the same conditions under which the oath is to be taken prevail.[62] In either event the oath is to be administered by the judge in the trial.[63] When a decisive oath taken during the progress of a trial relates to the principal matter in litigation, the trial concludes, for a settlement has been reached. Hence the *litis instantia* may be terminated with a decisive oath taken during the progress of a trial in settlement of the principal controversy in litigation.

A settlement by arbitration (*compromissum in arbitros*) is also effective in the concluding of the trial and judicial proceedings. By this form of settlement the opposing parties agree to commit their dispute to the judgment of one or several persons who are to decide the dispute according to the norms of law or according to the rules of equity.[64] From the dispute as decided according to the norms of law there remains the possibility of an appeal to the court wherein the cause would have been concluded normally. There is no appeal, however, when the dispute has been decided according to the rules of equity.[65] Again, as in the situation of the simple compromise, the civil laws of the respective countries are to be applied to these settlements reached by way of arbitration. Cer-

[59] Cf. canon 1835.

[60] Canon 1836, § 1, 3. If the oath is simply refused, it belongs to the judge to estimate the importance of this refusal, i.e., whether the refusal is based on good reasons or whether it is equivalent to a confession.

[61] Canon 1836, § 2; cf. also canons 1925 ff.

[62] Cf. canon 1935.

[63] Canon 1836, § 4-5.

[64] Canon 1929.

[65] Cf. Lega, *De Iudiciis Eccl.*, I, nn. 16-37.

tain causes[66] are excluded from this manner of settlement. Thus, the *litis instantia* is terminated when the trial is concluded by way of recourse to a settlement by arbitration.

A peremptory exception constitutes another way by which a trial may be concluded. A judicial action is the right to seek in trial what is one's due.[67] A judicial exception is an assertion made by one of the parties in litigation against the right of action of the other party by which the right of action of the other party in the trial may be retarded or definitely excluded.[68] Dilatory exceptions serve to impede for a time the exercise in the trial of a right of action,[69] whereas validly invoked peremptory exceptions, which put an end to litigation,[70] are absolute in the sense that they exclude the other party from the right of acting in the judicial forum in the particular cause at hand. These peremptory exceptions, which put an end to litigation, are proposed and ruled upon prior to the joinder of issue (*litis contestatio*). Such peremptory exceptions are, e. g., those which claim that the controversy has already been decided. Thus they exclude not only the action but also the process. Nevertheless, notwithstanding the general rule as to when exceptions are to be proposed, a peremptory exception even of this kind may be allowed consideration though it be proposed after the joinder of issue. In this latter event, however, the party who raised the exception is held liable for costs, unless he can prove that he did not wilfully delay the raising of the exception.[71] When an absolutely peremptory exception (*litis finitae exceptio*), i. e., one which excludes all further judicial procedure, is made during the trial and found to be legitimate, that trial will be concluded.[72]

Certain peremptory exceptions, i. e., simple peremptory exceptions, which directly attack the action but do not absolutely exclude all further proceedings, are to be raised after the joinder of issue. Such peremptory exceptions, e.g., exceptions charging mal-

[66] Cf. canon 1927.
[67] *Institutes* (4, 6) praemium.
[68] Beste, *Introductio*, p. 796.
[69] Cf. canon 1628, § 1.
[70] Cf. canon 1629, § 1.
[71] Canon 1629, § 1.
[72] Beste, *Introductio*, p. 797.

ice, fear, etc., are proposed in the probatory period of the trial, because they may be the only means left to the defendant for opposing and rejecting the proofs of the plaintiff.[73] These simply peremptory exceptions (*aliae exceptiones peremptoriae*) although of themselves they do not exclude all further procedure, do furnish the power to set aside the action brought by the adverse party. When a simple peremptory exception, e. g., an exception of legal prescription, is resolved favorably for the one who raised it in an incidental question, then further proceedings may come to a halt, thus concluding both the incidental instance and the instance of the trial as a whole. Hence the *litis instantia* is sometimes terminated by the operation of peremptory exceptions.

The trial is also concluded when the persons of the plaintiff and of the defendant become one and the same, e.g., during the course of the trial the defendant dies and from him the plaintiff inherits the object that was until then in litigation. The *litis instantia* also is thereupon concluded.[74]

Moreover, when the object of litigation is lost or so destroyed that not even its equivalent can be had, the trial becomes futile. By this indirect conclusion of the trial the *litis instantia* is terminated.[75]

When, during the progress of the trial, the plaintiff renounces his right to the action, the trial and the instance are concluded.[76]

Reiffenstuel stated that a trial may also end indirectly when during its progress it becomes evident to the judge that the bill of complaint as brought by the plaintiff has been ineptly drawn up.[77] Coronata declares that this circumstance is also effective and applicable in modern ecclesiastical law.[78] Thus, with the close of the trial in this manner the *litis instantia* also ends.

In summary, then, the *litis instantia* ends with the termination of the trial. The trial, however, is directly and normally concluded

[73] Beste, *loc. cit.*

[74] Coronata, *Institutiones*, III, p. 164, n. 1259.

[75] Lega-Bartoccetti, *Commentarius*, II, 566.

[76] Roberti, *De Processibus*, II, p. 4, footnote 1.

[77] *Ius Canonicum Universum*, Lib. II, tit. 1, n. 29.

[78] *Institutiones*, III, p. 164, footnote 7.

by means of the judicial sentence. The trial may also close abortively in consequence of the abatement of the instance (*peremptio instantiae*) or of the renunciation of the instance (*renuntiatio instantiae*). Among the other ways by which the trial concludes there can be enumerated the following: the contumacy of the plaintiff during the progress of the trial; the simple compromise (*transactio*) between the litigant parties which occurs during the trial; the decisive oath (*iusiurandum decisorium*), taken during the trial, which concludes the proceedings; the settlement by way of arbitration (*compromissum in arbitros*), which takes place during the course of the trial; the unification of the plaintiff and of the defendant into one and the same person; the loss or destruction of the object in litigation in such a way that no equivalent can be had in its place; the renunciation of the action itself by the plaintiff during the course of the trial, and when the bill of complaint (*libellus*) is found during the trial to be ineptly drawn up. Hence the trial may be concluded either directly or indirectly. Since the *litis instantia* closes in any of the ways by which the trial ends, the *litis instantia* may accordingly be terminated by any of the above mentioned methods.

The operation of the interruption of the lawsuit (*interruptio instantiae*), of the abatement of the lawsuit (*peremptio instantiae*), and of the renunciation of the lawsuit (*renuntiatio instantiae*) are institutes of law proper to the study of the *litis instantia*. Because of their direct importance to the *litis instantia*, the writer proposes to treat of them in the succeeding chapters as particular aspects of the *litis instantia*.

CHAPTER V

THE INTERRUPTION OF THE LITIS INSTANTIA

Article 1. The Notion of the Interruption of the Litis Instantia

The instance of a lawsuit is said to be interrupted when there occurs during the progress of the trial and before the closing of the cause (*conclusio in causa*) such a change in the condition of either of the litigant parties or of their proxies that they become physically or legally incapable of prosecuting their claims in the trial.[1] The interruption of the instance, however, is not the same as a suspension of the instance. The latter occurs when, because of some event not dependent on the status of the parties in the trial, the course of the proceedings is impeded.[2] The Code does not mention this distinction explicitly, but from its provisions on the subject of an interrupted instance[3] it is evident that only a juridical change in the status of the parties, their death, or the loss of the office by reason of which they acted in the trial, can effect the interruption of the instance. Hence, the suspension of the instance, which does not depend upon the juridical status, etc., of the parties involved in the trial, does not interrupt the instance in the legal sense.

Judicial exceptions relative to the competency of the judge in the trial,[4] exceptions of suspicion with reference to his unbiased interest in the cause,[5] pleas charging attempts prejudicial to the parties in contention while the litigation is pending (*attentata lite*

[1] Cf. canons 1733, 1735.

[2] Wernz-Vidal, *De Processibus*, p. 369, n. 410; Lega-Bartoccetti, *Commentarius*, II, 566-567; Roberti, *De Processibus*, II, p. 4, n. 308.

[3] Canons 1733, 1735.

[4] Canon 1610.

[5] Canons 1613-1617.

pendente),[6] and generally also all incidental questions cause a suspension of the principal instance of the cause when lodged during the progress of the trial.[7] Once these reasons for the suspension of the instance have been resolved, or also when they have automatically ceased, the instance continues as before; there is no need then for the formal resumption of the judicial proceedings.[8] It is not so in the interruption of the instance. A definite rupture in the proceedings (unless the *conclusio in causa* has already taken place) is caused by a change of the juridical status of the litigant parties or of their proxies in the trial. This rupture or interruption must be healed in order that the trial may proceed, i.e., the heir or the successor must fill the void caused by the death, juridical change or lapse from office of the original litigants involved. Hence, a formal resumption of the judicial proceedings becomes necessary.[9]

During the interruption of the instance the process cannot further evolve. Any judicial acts performed during the interim are affected with the stigma of nullity.[10] The trial remains pending and the lawsuit cannot be abated (*peremptio*), since a legal obstacle to further procedural acts is caused by the interruption.[11] The suspension of an instance, on the other hand, is subject to an abatement of the lawsuit since there is no legal obstacle to the performance of further procedural acts. Thus, it is true to say in a general, but not in a technical, sense that the *interruptio instantiae* causes a suspension of the judicial proceedings, since further proceedings are necessarily held in abeyance. This is not to say, however, that the suspension of the instance is the same as the interruption of the instance, since each has its own proper signification and effects. The Code says nothing explicitly with regard to the suspension of the instance, whereas the interruption of the instance is treated directly in canons 1733 and 1735.

[6] Canon 1854.

[7] Wernz-Vidal, *De Processibus*, p. 370, n. 410, footnote 5.

[8] Roberti, *De Processibus*, II, p. 4, n. 308; Wernz-Vidal, *loc. cit.*

[9] Roberti, *De Processibus*, II, p. 4, n. 309.

[10] Roberti, *loc. cit.*

[11] Cf. canon 1736.

Article 2. Causes Productive of the Interruption of the Instance on the Part of the Litigant

Canon 1733 speaks of the interruption of the instance as being caused by the death, the change of status, or the lapse from office[12] on the part of one of the litigant parties when the trial has not yet come to the closing of the cause (*conclusio in causa*). If the trial has progressed to the closing of the cause, neither death, nor change of status, nor lapse from office will interrupt the instance of the lawsuit. The judge is then to continue the cause by issuing a summons to the proxy, if there be one, or otherwise to the heir or the successor of the original litigant party.[13]

The closing of the cause (*conclusio in causa*) takes place whenever the parties questioned by the judge declare that they have nothing further to add, or whenever the time (a time available for use) fixed by the judge for the submission of proofs has elapsed, or when the judge declares that the cause has been sufficiently presented.[14] Thus, when everything that pertains to the probatory period of the trial has been fulfilled, the trial must come to the closing of the cause.[15] The Code rules that after the closing of the cause no new proofs are to be admitted, except in the causes which never become irrevocably adjudged, e.g., in marriage trials, or unless important documents pertaining to the cause have been newly discovered, or when witnesses could not previously be heard in view of some legitimate impediment.[16] Generally, then, after the closing of the cause no purpose would be served through the interruption of the proceedings.

[12] For the explanation of these concepts cf. *infra*, pp. 62-68.

[13] Canon 1733: Si pars litigans moriatur aut statum mutet aut cesset ab officio cuius ratione agit:

1° Causa nondum conclusa, instantia interrumpitur, donec heres defuncti aut successor litem instauret;

2° Causa conclusa, instantia non interrumpitur, sed iudex procedere debet ad ulteriora, citato procuratore, si adsit, secus defuncti herede vel successore.

[14] Canon 1860, § 2.

[15] Canon 1860, § 1.

[16] Canon 1861, § 1.

With regard to the interruption of the instance and the closing of the cause, therefore, two points must be remembered: the instance is interrupted if death, change of status, or lapse from office on the part of a litigant takes place while the trial is still in progress and has not reached the closing stage; the instance is not interrupted if the same events occur after the closing of the cause.[17] If death, change of status, or lapse from office occurs before the joinder of issue (*litis contestatio*), the instance cannot be interrupted for the simple reason that the *litis instantia* does not yet legally exist. To hold further proceedings when the events which are normally sufficient to cause an interruption occur before the joinder of issue, a new summons (*citatio*) is to be made to the heir or to the successor of the party who has been removed from the controversy so that they may undertake the litigation.[18]

When the instance is interrupted, i.e., when death, change of status, or lapse from office occurs before the closing of the cause, the judge or the tribunal declares the fact of this interruption by decree and notifies the adverse party in the trial of this fact.[19] It is evident that the same equitable procedure should be followed for the notification of the heirs or the successors of the litigant party when otherwise the heirs or the successors would remain unaware of the situation. The Code does not directly mention this procedure of notification either of the adverse party or of the heirs and the successors. Nevertheless, since the purpose of the *interruptio instantiae* is to concede to the litigant parties the means necessary for the defense of their rights,[20] and since the interruption will endure until the heir or the successor of the incapacitated party resumes the controversy,[21] this procedure must be considered implicit in the law of the Code. The adverse party can petition the

[17] If, however, an incidental question which must be judicially decided arises after the closing of the cause, this new phase of the process is subject to interruption, just as in the principal instance, until it reaches its own proper *conclusio in causa*. Cf. Roberti, *De Processibus*, II, p. 6, n. 310.

[18] *Ibid.*, p. 5, n. 310.

[19] *Loc. cit.*

[20] Coronata, *Institutiones*, III, p. 165, n. 1260.

[21] Canon 1733, 1°.

court to summon the heir or the successor to resume the instance, which summons, if it be left ultimately unheeded, can inject into the proceedings the challenging element of contumacy.[22]

The interrupted instance is considered resumed when the tribunal or the judge has been approached by the heir or the successor, and a notice has been sent to the adverse party in the cause.[23] Canon 1733, 1°, treats of the interrupted instance as being resumed by the heir or the successor of the incapacitated party. The heir or the successor resumes the instance by presenting a *libellus* to the judge (in marriage trials the judge will be the *ponens* in trials held by the Rota, and the *praeses* in other collegiate tribunals) in which *libellus* he proves his right of inheritance or of succession and asks to be admitted to continue the litigation. The presentation of this *libellus* is notified to the other party in the cause. If this party should challenge it, then there would arise a demand for the prior solution of the incidental question thus created.[24]

The *Dictionnaire de Droit Canonique* invokes canon 1655, § 2, in offering the opinion that the resumption of the instance can be taken *ex officio* by the judge in the trial.[25] Canon 1655, § 2, states that, when minors are involved in contentious trials, or when the cause affects the public welfare, the judge shall assign *ex officio* a defender to an undefended party. The writer is in accord with the opinion offered in the *Dictionnaire,* provided that the litigant party remains otherwise defenseless, even as minors lack a defense, or, that the issue at trial involves the public welfare. If, however, this opinion is meant to include any and every cause as implicitly involving the public welfare and therefore as lending itself to a resumption *ex officio* by the judge, then the writer must demur. The resumption of such causes belongs by right to the lawful heirs or the successors. Should these choose to relinquish their rights, that is their privilege. Should they default by non-

[22] Coronata, *Institutiones,* III, p. 166, n. 1260; Roberti, *De Processibus,* II, p. 6, n. 310; Cf. also canons 1844, 1850.

[23] Coronata, *Institutiones,* III, p. 165, n. 1260.

[24] Pinna, *Praxis Iudicialis Canonica* (Romae: Officium Libri Catholici, 1952), p. 45; *Normae Sacrae Romanae Rotae,* Art. 79, § 1-2 — *AAS,* XXVI (1934), 470.

[25] *Dictionnaire,* IV, 1441.

action, legal remedies such as proceedings in contumacy can be invoked by the adverse party.[26]

The causes productive of the *interruptio instantiae* on the part of the litigant are exhaustively (*taxative,* i.e., completely) enumerated in canon 1733.[27] Hence, with regard to the litigant (as distinct from the proxy, of whom canon 1735 treats), only death, change of status, or lapse from office effects the interruption of the instance. It will be of profit to explore each of these three factors in detail.

A. The Death of the Litigant Party

The death of a litigant party obviously removes him from further controversy. When the death of a litigant party occurs before the closing of the cause, only the heir or the successor has the right to fill his place in the trial, since these alone possess the rights of inheritance or succession.[28] If the deceased litigant used the services of a proxy in the trial, that proxy can, at most, act only to inform the court of the death of his principal, in order that the court may decree the interruption of the instance and notify the adverse party of this fact. Coronata[29] states that, should this proxy be unaware of the death of his principal and should he thus continue to act in the trial when the closing of the cause has not yet been reached, his acts would be of no avail, completely null and void.[30]

The dissolution of a moral personality[31] is similar to the death of a physical person in this regard.[32] By the death of a physical person in litigation the rights as exercised by him pass to another, i.e., to his heir or the successor. So also with the dissolution of the moral personality[33] in litigation. The only questions which arise

[26] Cf. canons 1849, 1850 and 1844 ff.

[27] Coronata, *Institutiones,* III, p. 166, n. 1260.

[28] Cf. canon 1733, 1°; Wernz-Vidal, *De Processibus,* p. 370, n. 411.

[29] *Institutiones,* III, p. 165, n. 1260.

[30] Cf., however, Regolamento Legislativo, Sezione V, § 903, where in pre-Code legislation the proxy could legally act for a deceased litigant.

[31] Canon 102.

[32] Roberti, *De Processibus,* II, p. 5, n. 310.

[33] Cf. canon 102, § 1.

are whether there is a succession and, if so, which personality succeeds to the rights of the "deceased" moral personality.[84]

In marriage causes involving the alleged nullity of the marriage, if it is ascertained from authentic documents during the course of the trial and before the pronouncement of the sentence that either one of the consorts has died, the acts of the cause are to be placed in the court archives. No decision is to be rendered, even though the trial be past the closing stage of the cause (*causa iam conclusa*), unless the other consort or an heir of the deceased insists that a definitive sentence in the cause be reached.[85]

In a recent Rotal decision (July 22, 1953)[86] a clarification of the meaning of the term "heir" was given a practical solution. The question at stake involved the death of the appellant party during the pendency of an appeal from an adverse judgment relative to the nullity of the marriage. The parents of the deceased appellant were allowed to prosecute the appeal. It was ruled that the term "heir" is not limited to the principal heir at law, but may include also other persons who have a serious interest in the case, e.g., for reasons of an economic nature.

It is noteworthy that when the controversy is non-transferable, e.g., a petition for separation from bed and board, the death of a litigant party does not interrupt the instance but rather concludes the trial,[87] since there is truly nothing left that is open to contest. In this event it can well be said: *mors enim omnia solvit.*

B. Change of Juridical Status

The status of a person is said to be changed when the person enters upon a way of life in which until then he had not been a participant. This change of status, however, will not effect an interruption of the instance unless it be such a juridical change that it bears a real influence on the litigation involved.[88] Not every

[84] Cf. Lega-Bartoccetti, *Commentarius,* II, 568.

[85] S.C. de Sacramentis, *Instructio* (15 Augusti, 1936), Art. 222, § 1 — *AAS,* XXVIII (1936), 357.

[86] Reported in *The Canon Law Digest, Annual Supplement through 1954* (Bouscaren-O'Connor) under canon 1733.

[87] Roberti, *De Processibus,* II, p. 6, n. 310.

[88] Coronata, *Institutiones,* III, p. 166, n. 1260.

change will effect an interruption of the instance therefore. Only such juridical changes in the persons involved in the litigation as affect the rights or the capacity of the litigants to have a standing in the trial can produce the *interruptio instantiae.*[39] For example, parents or guardians act as the representatives of minors in litigation.[40] When the minor reaches adult age, he is capable of representing himself and should do so. In this latter circumstance a juridical change has occurred, since the minor has now become legally able to represent himself, and this juridical change has a real bearing on the controversy being litigated. So, also, canon 1652 sets the general norm that religious are not to be involved in litigation unless they have the approval of their superiors. Hence, a party in litigation, if in the interim he becomes a religious, undergoes a juridical change in his status which is pertinent to the judicial proceedings.

What occurs if a litigant party becomes insane? In this circumstance canons 88, § 3, and 1648, § 1, provide the solution. In their juridical status insane persons are likened to infants.[41] Parents and guardians are to act in litigation for minors and for those who are destitute of reason.[42] Thus, the question of insanity involves a real juridical change in status, since an adult thereby becomes legally equivalent to an infant.

Does excommunication produce this juridical change of status? Canon 1654 rules that those who are formally excommunicated as persons who are to be shunned (*excommunicati vitandi*) and those whose excommunication has been declared or inflicted by way of a sentence (*excommunicati tolerati post sententiam declaratoriam vel condemnatoriam*) are permitted to act as litigants in the ecclesiastical courts only with a view to impugning the justice or legitimacy of their excommunication. To avert any other spiritual harm they may act through a proxy. In all other causes, however, they are not to be admitted as litigants in the ecclesiastical courts.

[39] Wernz-Vidal, *De Processibus*, p. 371, n. 411; Roberti, *De Processibus*, II, p. 5, n. 310.

[40] Canon 1648, § 1.

[41] Canon 88, § 3.

[42] Canon 1648, § 1.

Other excommunicated persons, i.e., those who are not *vitandi*, or those whose excommunication is not signalized by way of a declaratory or condemnatory sentence, are generally admitted as plaintiffs in ecclesiastical courts.

With canon 1654 as a basis, an opinion has gained sway that these other simply excommunicated persons may be plaintiffs in court until the exception of excommunication is raised against them.[48] In other words, it is claimed that canon 1654, § 2, is modified by canon 1628, § 3, which states that the exception of excommunication can be raised at every period and every stage of the trial, provided it be raised before the final sentence. In the case of *excommunicati vitandi* or *excommunicati tolerati post sententiam declaratoriam vel condemnatoriam* the same law rules that these must always be excluded *ex officio* by the court itself. Does canon 1628, § 3, therefore, complement canon 1654 in the sense that simply excommunicated persons, who generally are admissible in the ecclesiastical courts, would be devoid of the right to stand in trial if an exception is lodged against them? Or is it that canon 1628, § 3, speaks rather of the time period in which exceptions are to be raised, and therefore is not directly concerned with the substantive law on the *ius standi in iudicio* of excommunicated persons? It is the opinion of the present writer that the latter supposition is the correct one, and that accordingly it is canon 2263 in conjunction with canon 1654, § 2, that enacts the basic substantive law on the rôle of simply excommunicated persons in ecclesiastical trials.

Canon 2263 rules that an excommunicated person is forbidden to exercise legally authorized ecclesiastical acts within the limits defined in law, that he cannot be a plaintiff in ecclesiastical trials *except in so far as canon 1654 permits,* and that he is forbidden to discharge ecclesiastical offices and duties or to enjoy privileges previously granted to him by the Church. It is felt, then, that in the question of the right of simply excommunicated persons to stand in trial canon 2263 should be considered as basic, that it is

[48] Woywod-Smith, *Practical Commentary,* II, 258; Coyle, *Judicial Exceptions,* The Catholic University of America Canon Law Studies, n. 193 (Washington, D. C.: The Catholic University of America Press, 1944), pp. 106-107.

complemented by canon 1654, § 2, and that only then should consideration be given to canon 1628, § 3, with reference namely to the time element in which exceptions of excommunication are to be raised. With such an explanation the force of canon 1654, § 2, which states that simply excommunicated persons can generally stand in trial, will not be weakened.

The objection that the *generatim stare in iudicio* of canon 1654, § 2, makes allowance for an exception of excommunication even in regard to those who are simply excommunicated one can answer by pointing out the fact that proxies and advocates duly appointed to act for a plaintiff in a trial may also be subject to the penalty of excommunication. It is against these and such others as guardians, curators, or administrators active in a representative capacity, that the *generatim stare in iudicio* of canon 1654, § 2, in conjunction with canon 2263 refers, and it is against such that the exception of simple excommunication may be raised. These proxies, advocates, and others, perform legally authorized ecclesiastical acts in ecclesiastical trials. But, simply excommunicated persons are by canon 2263 forbidden to perform legally authorized ecclesiastical acts. Thus, proxies, advocates and such others who have fallen under the penalty of simple excommunication are forbidden to act in ecclesiastical trials. Hence, the sense of canon 1654, § 2, is that simply excommunicated persons generally have the right to stand in trial unless they are acting in some representative capacity in the trial. Simple excommunication, therefore, does not change the juridical status of the *principal litigant* in the trial.

C. Lapse from Office

If a person loses the office in virtue of which he is taking part in the trial, that person is no longer competent to act in behalf of the office he formerly represented. Obviously, one cannot be the representative of something which is no longer in one's possession. Official representatives of moral personalities, such as pastors representing parishes, rectors representing seminaries, etc.,[44] may die,

[44] Cf. Wernz-Vidal, *De Processibus*, p. 371, n. 411; Coronata, *Institutiones*, III, p. 166, n. 1260.

be removed from, or renounce the office they hold.[45] Such persons, then, no longer represent the office in behalf of which they formerly acted. They cannot continue to act in the trial in their former capacity. When such a lapse from office occurs before the closing of the cause in the trial, the instance of the lawsuit is interrupted. The successors to these offices attain the right of representation, and it is to them that the resumption of an interrupted instance belongs.

By virtue of canon 1653, § 5, local ordinaries may appear in court either in person or through another to act for moral personalities under their jurisdiction whenever these moral personalities are without a representative either because of the neglect of the legally determined representative, or because of the lack of such a representative. Thus, the resumption of an interrupted instance can be activated by local ordinaries in trials concerned with moral personalities under their jurisdiction whenever the representatives of these moral personalities do not or cannot act.

Since the office and not the person is to be considered with regard to the promoter of justice and the defender of the bond, the *litis instantia* will not be legally interrupted even if the office is not at the time filled. The proceedings, however, do not progress until a new promoter of justice or defender of the bond has been appointed.[46]

In summary, then, except for the office of the promoter of justice or of the defender of the bond, a lapse from office on the part of the person who previously represented that office effects an interruption of the instance when the closing of the cause in the trial has not yet been reached.

The following are the basic provisions of canon 1733. The interruption of the instance will not occur when the closing of the cause (*conclusio in causa*) has taken place. When the closing of the cause has taken place, the judge continues with the trial by issuing a summons to the proxy if there be one, or otherwise to the heir or the successor of the incapacitated litigant party. When the closing of the cause has not yet occurred, the instance will be interrupted

[45] Cf. canon 183, § 1.

[46] Roberti, *De Processibus*, II, p. 5, n. 310.

when a litigant party dies, suffers a pertinent juridical change in his status, or ceases to act in behalf of the office which he represented in the trial. No interruption of the instance can occur when the joinder of issue has not yet been effected even equivalently. The instance obviously cannot be interrupted if it does not yet exist.

Article 3. The Interruption of the Instance on the Part of Proxies and Guardians

If a proxy or a guardian ceases to act for his client, the lawsuit remains interrupted until the client or the persons concerned have appointed a new proxy or a guardian, or have declared that they will personally prosecute the cause.[47]

Does canon 1735 establish a norm of procedure different from that of canon 1733 in regard to the interruption of the instance, or is it rather a canon explanatory of the length of time the instance may remain interrupted when proxies or guardians die or lose their office?

A strong argument militates for those[48] who maintain that canons 1733 and 1735 differ in their effects. First, of what necessity would canon 1735 be if it were substantially the same as canon 1733? Could its reference to proxies be not just as well made in canon 1733? Moreover, why the separation of canons 1733 and 1735 by an intervening canon, which speaks of a matter in which no interruption of the instance occurs, unless canons 1733 and 1735 do differ substantially? Roberti[49] states that the interruption of the instance in each canon is ruled by its own norms and produces its own effects. Both Roberti and Pinna[50] observe that, even though the proxies die or lose their office after the closing of the cause in the trial (*conclusio in causa*), the instance will be interrupted. It

[47] Canon 1735: Procuratore aut curatore a munere cessante, tandiu interrupta manet instantia, quandiu pars aut ii ad quos pertinet novum procuratorem vel curatorem nominaverint aut per se ipsi in posterum agere se velle professi fuerint.

[48] Roberti, *De Processibus*, II, p. 7, n. 311; Pinna, *Praxis Iudicialis*, p. 47.

[49] *Loc. cit.*

[50] *Loc. cit.*

must be admitted that canon 1735 states nothing explicitly about the closing of the cause in reference to the *interruptio instantiae.* On the other hand, it may be argued that, since canon 1733 treats of those persons who effect the interruption of the instance through their lapse from the office in virtue of which they act in the trial, it is substantially the same as canon 1735, which treats of the cessation of the rôle of proxies and guardians. Thus, Roberti admits that the rôle of guardians already is treated under canon 1733.[51]

Coronata observes that the reading of canon 1733 makes no explicit reference to the death or change of status of proxies. Nevertheless, he says, canon 1733 implicitly includes them since the proxy, although strictly not to be identified with the litigant party, nevertheless acts in the name and under the authority of the litigant party.[52] Hence, in regard to the interruption of the instance, canon 1735 is not basically different from canon 1733.

Perhaps a stronger support for the opinion of Roberti and Pinna could be derived from a consideration of the phrase, *aut cesset ab officio,* in canon 1733. If canon 1733 referred to an *ecclesiastical* office in its use of the word office, then it would be very plausible that a substantial difference between canons 1733 and 1735 exists. Canon 145, § 1, defines the ecclesiastical office in two senses. In the broad sense of the term, an ecclesiastical office is any employment which is legitimately practiced for a spiritual purpose. In the strict sense, an ecclesiastical office means a permanently fixed position created either by the divine or the ecclesiastical law, conferred according to the rules of the sacred canons, and entailing at least some participation in ecclesiastical power whether of orders or of jurisdiction.[53] Canon 145, § 2, states that in law the term "ecclesiastical

[51] *De Processibus,* II, p. 7, n. 311: "Codex hic loquitur de 'procuratore aut curatore' (c. 1735). At curator propria ratione comprehenditur inter eos qui 'ratione officii' agunt in canone 1733 . . . ."

[52] *Institutiones,* III, p. 166, n. 1260.

[53] Canon 145, § 1: Officium ecclesiasticum lato sensu est quodlibet munus quod in spiritualem finem legitime exercetur; stricto autem sensu est munus ordinatione sive divina sive ecclesiastica stabiliter constitutum, ad normam sacrorum canonum conferendum, aliquam saltem secumferens participationem ecclesiasticae potestatis sive ordinis sive iurisdictionis.

office" is used in its strict sense unless the context indicates otherwise.[54]

If the *cesset ab officio* in canon 1733 refers to an ecclesiastical office, then it should be taken in the strict sense of an ecclesiastical office, since no further qualification of this term is made in canon 1733. Thus, only those who in some manner hold ecclesiastical power, such as pastors, or religious superiors of clerical houses, would be spoken of in canon 1733. The term *curator* in canon 1735, would then accordingly refer to someone less than a person possessing an ecclesiastical office in the strict sense, e.g., the lay guardian of some person. In the light of this explanation, the *cesset ab officio* in canon 1733 would refer to persons possessing an ecclesiastical office in the strict sense, and the *curatore cessante a munere* in canon 1735 would refer to those persons who do not possess an ecclesiastical office in the strict sense. A substantial difference between canons 1733 and 1735 could, perhaps, be thus argued as plausible.

Notwithstanding this reasoning the writer holds that canons 1733 and 1735 are substantially the same, not differing in their effects. The Code does not distinguish its terminology in the sense to which the opposite opinion subscribes. Moreover, it seems gratuitous to say that canon 1735 does not really intend to speak of *curatores* but only of proxies. The fact of the matter is that canon 1735 does mention *curatores* expressly.[55] It seems, then, that the more acceptable opinion is the one which maintains that canons 1733 and 1735 are substantially the same.

When the proxy or the guardian ceases to act for his client, the instance of the lawsuit will be interrupted if the closing of the cause has not yet occurred. The instance will remain interrupted until the litigant party or those to whom it belongs to appoint a new proxy or guardian have appointed him or have signified that they will thenceforth prosecute the cause personally.[56] The observations made in canon 1733 regarding the resumption of the *litis*

[54] Canon 145, § 2: In iure officium ecclesiasticum accipitur stricto sensu, nisi aliud ex contextu sermonis appareat.

[55] Canon 1735: . . . procuratore aut *curatore* a munere cessante. . . .

[56] Canon 1735.

instantia should be accepted as applicable also for the situation contemplated in canon 1735.[57]

It should be noted from the commentary in the preceding article that an exception of excommunication may be raised against a proxy, which exception, if found true, would exclude him from further acting in the cause.

The appointment of the new proxy or the new guardian is communicated to the court and is made known to the adverse party in the trial. If the one to whom the appointment pertains fails, either to make the appointment or to prosecute the cause himself, the adverse party can request the court to set a peremptory time limit within which the delinquent litigant must act or otherwise reap the consequence of proceedings in contumacy.[58] When the proxy ceases to act in the cause even prior to the joinder of issue, no interruption of the instance occurs, since the *litis instantia* does not yet exist. So also, when the closing of the cause in the trial has already taken place, no interruption occurs in accordance with the provisions of canon 1733.

Article 4. Litigation over the Right to a Benefice

In canon 1734 an exception to the general rule with regard to the interruption of the instance is made. If there is a controversy between two clerics over the right to a benefice, and one of the litigants dies while the cause is pending,[59] or one resigns his right to the benefice, the instance of the lawsuit[60] is not interrupted, but the promoter of justice conducts the cause against the survivor in behalf of the liberty of the benefice or of the Church, unless the benefice is one which the ordinary can freely confer and which he

[57] Canon 1733: Si pars litigans moriatur aut statum mutet aut cesset ab officio cuius ratione agit:

1° Causa nondum conclusa, instantia interrumpitur, donec heres defuncti aut successor litem instauret;

2° Causa conclusa, instantia non interrumpitur, sed iudex procedere debet ad ulteriora, citato procuratore, si adsit, secus defuncti herede vel successore.

[58] Roberti, *De Processibus*, II, p. 7, n. 311.

[59] Cf. canon 1725. The cause begins to pend when the summons has been served.

[60] Cf. canon 1732. The instance of the lawsuit begins with the joinder of issue.

wishes to confer to the surviving party, as to the one who won his suit.[61] This exception to the general norm for the interruption of the instance is made lest ecclesiastical benefices be conferred without canonical appointment[62] by the competent ecclesiastical authority.[63]

An ecclesiastical benefice is a perpetual juridical institute set up or established by competent ecclesiastical authority, and consisting of a sacred office and of the right to receive the income from the endowment attached to that office.[64] No ecclesiastical office can be obtained without a provision canonical in character.[65] No ecclesiastical benefice, therefore, can be obtained without a similar canonical provision, since the basic constituent of the ecclesiastical benefice is the ecclesiastical office itself. By canonical provision is meant the concession of an ecclesiastical office made by a competent ecclesiastical authority according to the norms of Canon law.[66] Canon 148 treats of the manner in which appointment to ecclesiastical office may ensue. Thus, the free conferment (*libera collatio*) of an office, the grant of title given subsequent to a nomination made by one possessing the right of patronage (*ius patronatus*),[67] the confirmation of an election by the competent superior, admission granted to one postulated for an office,[68] and simple election to an office which needs only the acceptance of the one elected, are the different ways in which an appointment to an ecclesiastical office may be effected.

[61] Canon 1734: Si controvertatur cuinam ex clericis litigantibus ius sit ad beneficium, et alter, lite pendente, moriatur, aut beneficio renuntiet, instantia non interrumpitur, sed contra superstitem eam prosequitur promotor iustitiae qui pro beneficii aut ecclesiae libertate dimicet, nisi beneficium sit liberae collationis Ordinarii et hic praeferat causam ut victam superstiti adiudicare.

[62] Cf. canon 147.

[63] Coronata, *Institutiones,* III, p. 167, n. 1260.

[64] Canon 1409.

obtained without a provision canonical in character.[65] No ecclesias-

[65] Canon 147, § 1.

[66] Canon 147, § 2.

[67] Cf. canons 1448 ff.

[68] Postulation of a candidate establishes no right as such to the office. Cf. canon 181, § 3.

When different clerics contend that each of them has a right to a benefice to the exclusion of the others as having been established by free conferment, presentation, nomination, or by election, that benefice is said to be under litigation.[69] Thus, a person who has a legitimate title to obtain the possession of a certain thing, or the exercise of a certain right, may petition the ecclesiastical court that he be granted the possession of such a thing or the exercise of such a right.[70] A real action obtains in court, therefore, when a litigant cleric contends that a benefice is his by legitimate title. If the litigant cleric contends only that he has the right to be presented or to be elected, this constitutes only a *personal* action on his part, since the matter at issue is not the right to the benefice itself. The sense of canon 1734, therefore, refers to litigation as based on a *real* action, the right to a benefice as by title, and not, therefore, merely the right to be presented, to be elected, etc.[71]

In the middle ages there had been two precise provisions in this matter. Boniface VIII (1294-1303) had prescribed that, once the cause was pending, the surviving litigant would not thereby succeed to the benefice if the other litigant cleric died or gave up the litigation.[72] Somewhat later, probably in the reign of Pope John XXII (1316-1334),[73] the rule of Boniface VIII was modified somewhat, so that the surviving cleric in litigation could succeed to the rights of the non-contesting or deceased adverse cleric. This later rule was made lest litigation in this matter be prolonged indefinitely.[74] Under this later rule one month was allowed the surviving litigant cleric to seek apostolic letters of confirmation, so that he might succeed to the benefice.[75]

Today, the Code rules that, when the benefice under litigation is one which the ordinary may freely confer, he may if he so prefers

[69] Lega-Bartoccetti, *Commentarius,* II, 571.

[70] Cf. canon 1693.

[71] Cf. Lega-Bartoccetti, *Commentarius,* II, 571-572.

[72] C. 1, *ut lite pendente nihil innovetur,* II, 5, in Clem.

[73] Cf. Lega-Bartoccetti, *Commentarius,* II, 570, who speak of Pope John XXIII but evidently they mean to refer to Pope John XXII (1316-1334) and not to the anti-pope John XXIII (1410-1415).

[74] Lega-Bartoccetti, *loc. cit.*

[75] Cf. Roberti, *De Processibus,* II, p. 6, n. 310, footnote 1.

confer it on the surviving litigant. When the benefice under litigation is not one which can be freely conferred, the promoter of justice is to prosecute the litigation against the surviving litigant on behalf of the liberty of the benefice. When the benefice under litigation is one which can indeed be freely conferred, but which the ordinary is disinclined to confer, the promoter of justice is to act for the freedom of the benefice. In any event, it is to be remembered that the *litis instantia* does not suffer a legal interruption in these circumstances. Obviously, the proceedings are terminated if the ordinary freely confers a benefice when he has the power to do so. When the proceedings are continued, however, the judge issues a summons to the promoter of justice, even though the cause has not yet reached the stage at which the joinder of issue is effected.[76]

[76] *Loc. cit.*

CHAPTER VI

THE ABATEMENT (PEREMPTIO) OF THE INSTANCE

Article 1. Notion of the Abatement of the Instance

The abatement or discharge of the instance of a lawsuit consists in the extinction of the judicial process due to the prolonged inactivity of the litigant parties.[1] This discharge of the instance so affects the process that the litigant parties may no longer continue or reinstitute the same proceedings.[2] This is not to say that the cause in dispute may not again be brought to trial. It does mean, however, that, if the cause is to continue, then judicial proceedings must be begun again as though there had never been a previous process. Hence, the abatement of the instance differs from the effective legal prescription that quashes a judicial action. The abatement extinguishes that particular process in which the action is being tried, but it does not extinguish the action itself. Although the instance (and the judicial process as a whole) becomes extinct, the action may be brought in a new process. Good faith on the part of the parties is not a requisite for the abatement. The agency of legal prescription, on the other hand, demands this good faith as a postulate for the quashing of the trial.[3]

Ancient Roman law and the provisions of pre-Code Canon law maintained the abatement of an instance, but in a mode somewhat different from the Canon law of today.[4] Roman law and the former Canon law based their concept of the abatement of the instance (*peremptio instantiae*) on considerations of the public good (*ne*

[1] Roberti, *De Processibus,* II, p. 10, n. 313.

[2] Coronata, *Institutiones,* III, p. 167, n. 1261.

[3] Cf. canon 1512.

[4] Gaius (4, 104-105); *Codex* (3, 1) 13; c. 20, X, *de iudiciis,* II, 1; c. 5, X, *De appellationibus, recusationibus et relationibus,* II, 28; cc. 3, 6, 7, *de appellationibus,* II, 12, in Clem.; Council of Trent Sess. XXIV, *de ref.,* c. 20. See also the historical conspectus, pp. 9-11, 14-16, 19-21, 23-28.

lites fiant immortales) and as a punitive inducement to forestall the inactivity of negligent litigants. Modern ecclesiastical law views the abatement of the instance from the aspect of a tacit renunciation of the instance by the parties involved.[5] Thus, no abatement of the instance occurs when there is an obstacle to impede further procedural action.[6] When no obstacle exists, a tacit renunciation of the instance is presumed in virtue of the prolonged inactivity of the litigant parties.[7]

Present ecclesiastical law seeks to avoid the two extreme consequences, suffered under Roman law and pre-Code law, which were so detrimental to the efficient movement of a judicial process. To avoid the procedural evil of an excessively prolonged trial the old law fell into the opposite fault, the insufficiency of time for a thorough investigation and deliberation of the litigated issue. In reaction to this state of affairs, ecclesiastical legislation swung back to the opposite extreme. The abatement of the instance was outlawed in practice.[8] Canonical legislation for the efficient movement of judicial proceedings seemed caught in a dilemna. The law today avoids both of these extremes. It avoids the evils of a prolonged process and of its opposite counterpart, the insufficiency of time for a proper juridical evaluation, by determining that an abatement of the instance will take effect when no procedural act has been placed for two years in a court which conducts the initial hearing, or for one year in a court of appeal, unless there has been an obstacle to impede such procedural acts.[9]

Article 2. Conditions Producing the Abatement of the Instance

Canon 1620 admonishes ecclesiastical tribunals and the judges thereof to expedite as soon as possible, *salva iustitia,* all lawsuits under their jurisdiction, and states that these causes should not be

[5] Wernz-Vidal, *De Processibus,* p. 373, n. 412.

[6] Canon 1736.

[7] Roberti, *De Processibus,* II, p. 10, n. 313.

[8] C. 20, X, *de iudiciis, II,* 1.

[9] Cf. the commentary below on canon 1736.

protracted over two years in courts of a first hearing or over one year in courts of a second or later hearing. Canon 1736 regulates the conditions which produce the abatement of an instance. When, in the absence of an obstacle, no procedural act has been placed for two years in a court of first hearing or for one year in a court of appeal, the instance of a lawsuit shall be discharged and, with reference to a court of appeal, the appealed sentence shall become a *res iudicata,* irrevocably adjudged.[10] From the aforementioned canons the law's intent is evident: lawsuits should not exceed a two-year period, or even a one-year period when there is question of an appellate court. In canon 1620, the courts are the subject of the law's concern. Canon 1736 implies this warning to the litigant parties themselves, and declares the consequence of the failure to observe the set time period. The abatement of the instance, therefore, is more than a result of a mere presumption of tacit renunciation. The law holds it equivalent to a tacit renunciation. The only proof which could forestall the effects of the abatement of an instance would have to derive from evidence that a legitimate obstacle impeded the observance of the stated time period.

Three conditions may be enumerated which together produce the abatement of an instance: 1) no procedural act was placed; 2) no legitimate obstacle impeded procedural action; 3) this procedural inactivity existed for two years in a court of first hearing, or for one year in a court of appeal.

Procedural acts should be understood here as acts placed in the judicial process by either of the litigant parties in opposition to the other's interests, i.e., as acts which further the position or enhance the arguments of one of the litigants as against the position or arguments of the other.[11] In other words, the acts of a judge alone cannot prevent the abatement of the instance, because the

[10] Canon 1736: Si nullus actus processualis, quin aliquod obstet impedimentum, ponatur in tribunali primae instantiae per biennium aut in gradu appellationis per annum, instantia perimitur, et in altero casu sententia per appellationem oppugnata transit in rem iudicatam.

No *res iudicata* is, of course, possible in marriage causes dealing with the status of persons. Cf. canon 1903.

[11] Lega-Bartoccetti, *Commentarius,* II, 584.

abatement should not and does not depend upon the choice of the judge.[12] It is from the last procedural act placed by the litigant parties in the process that the computation of the time period for a possible abatement of the instance is to be made.[13]

A procedural act which is null and void does not suffice to prevent the abatement of the instance. What is of no value produces no effect.[14] If, however, the act which is null be approved and admitted by the opponent, i.e., the adverse litigant party, then that act will be considered sanated and the abatement of the instance will be prevented.[15]

A legitimate obstacle impeding further procedural acts suffices to forestall the abatement of the instance. The abatement of an instance, therefore, cannot occur during a legitimate interruption (*interruptio instantiae*) of that instance. If a litigant party is unable to act when by law he is called upon to do so, then no abatement of the instance can take place. The Code, however, does not make the status of a person who is still in his minority to be an impediment.[16] Hence, while canon 1736 deals with an impediment as forestalling the abatement of the instance, canon 1737 invokes an exception to this rule, i.e., the status of a person in his minority does not constitute such an impediment. Aside from this exception, it devolves upon the judge to estimate the legitimacy of an

[12] Cf. canon 1618; to the contrary, cf. Roberti, *De Processibus*, II, p. 11, n. 314, where he states that, whether the acts placed in the process be of the parties or of the judge, they suffice to bar an abatement. Nevertheless, immediately thereupon Roberti states that the abatement cannot depend upon the will of the judge. If, however, the judge can perform a procedural act which in itself suffices to bar the abatement, is this not to say that the abatement of the instance can be forestalled at his will?

[13] Lega-Bartoccetti, *loc. cit.*

[14] Cf. Roberti, *De Processibus*, II, p. 11, n. 314; Lega-Bartoccetti, *Commentarius*, II, 584; Regula 64, *R. J.* in VI°: "Quae contra ius fiunt, debent utique pro infectis haberi," from which comes the modern equivalent: "Quod nullum est nullum producit effectum"; to the contrary, cf. Coronata, *Institutiones*, III, p. 168, n. 1262, footnote 1, where he says that we should imitate civil laws in this matter. Hence, in the opinion of Coronata, although an act be of itself null, it will remain a procedural act so long as it reflects the proper legal form.

[15] Lega-Bartoccetti, *loc. cit.*; Roberti, *loc. cit.*

[16] Cf. canon 1737.

impediment to procedural action. This is implicit in the very reading of canon 1737, in accord with which the judge must even *ex officio* sometimes declare the abatement of the instance.[17] It is the opinion of the writer that such an obstacle will exist when inculpable ignorance or the inability to act forestalls the exercise or the prosecution of one's rights. Hence, the standard or norm by which the judge will decide the legitimacy of an obstacle to judicial procedure should be sought within the legal framework of available time as defined in canon 35.[18] Thus, an impediment to procedural action which is deliberately created by either of the litigant parties should not suffice to bar the abatement of the instance.[19]

Procedural inactivity of the parties when extending for two years in courts of a first hearing or for one year in appellate courts, will produce, in the absence of a legitimate impediment, the abatement of an instance. This indicated span of time, then, is to be considered as a span of available time.[20] Hence, for one unable to act or inculpably ignorant of his duty to act, no lapse of time will operate in favor of the later abatement of the instance. The day on which the last procedural act was placed is not counted in the computation of the temporal span but the expiration of this span of time ensues upon the completed lapse of the day that marks the closing date of the two-or one-year period.[21] When there is no interruption in the continued lapse of time, then the computation is reckoned in line with the calendar year itself.[22] When some legitimate obstacle to the computable lapse of time occurs, the year should be reckoned as consisting of 365 whole days.[23] The time which lapses in the face of an obstacle is not to be computed as lapsing time.[24]

[17] Cf. Lega-Bartoccetti, *Commentarius*, II, 586.

[18] Canon 35: Tempus *utile* illud intelligitur quod pro exercitio aut prosecutione sui iuris ita alicui competit ut ignoranti aut agere non valenti non currat; *continuum*, quod nullam patitur interruptionem.

[19] To the contrary, cf. Coronata, *Institutiones*, III, p. 168, n. 1262.

[20] Cf. canon 35.

[21] Cf. canon 34, § 3, 3°.

[22] Cf. canon, 34, § 3, 1°.

[23] Cf. canon 35 in conjunction with canon 32, § 2.

[24] Roberti, (*De Processibus*, II, p. 11, n. 314) refers to canon 34, § 2, for the computation of time when an obstacle exists.

The *terminus a quo*, that is, the procedural act which marks the point from which the accumulated lapse of time for the abatement of the instance draws its origin, is the last procedural act that was placed subsequent to the joinder of issue.[25] Although the decree of summons (*citatio*) issued by the court at the behest of the plaintiff is truly a procedural act, nevertheless it does not mark the inception of the instance of the lawsuit, for the period of prosecution in the trial begins only after a joining of the issue.[26] The law deals with the abatement of the instance of the lawsuit. With the abatement of the instance, the procedural acts previous to it are also discharged. It does not follow, however, that the discharge of the summons along with other procedural acts which follow upon the joinder of issue (*litis contestatio*) will let the lapse of time that leads to the abatement of the instance start its computation from the time of the summons itself. Lega-Bartoccetti argue that the computation of the lapse of time that leads to the abatement of the instance may commence from the issuance of the summons. The present writer finds no reason for disagreement when they state that the summons is an *actus processualis*. He admits, also, that the abatement of the instance extinguishes the *acta processus*, and hence also the summons. But his accord with these authors does not extend beyond this point. Lega-Bartoccetti, in continuing their argument, claim that the abatement of the instance would not extinguish the summons if the latter was not included as part of the instance itself. It may simply be observed here that the summons is extinguished, not because it is part of the instance (it is not such a part), but because it is a procedural act. Lega-Bartoccetti state that, although the instance of the lawsuit properly and formally begins with the joinder of issue, effectively and virtually it begins with the summons (*citatio*), since therein it has its root. Hence, so Lega-Bartoccetti claim, the abatement of the instance looks to the issuance of the summons as the starting point from which the lapse of the two-or one-year period of time may be computed.[27]

[25] Roberti, *loc. cit.*

[26] Cf. canon 1732.

[27] *Commentarius*, II, 583, 589. Canon 254 of the Oriental law on procedure, however, does give support to this opinion. Cf. *Litterae Apostolicae Motu Proprio*

The law, however, clearly makes the commencement of the instance to coincide temporally with the joinder of issue.[28] The law expressly also treats of the abatement of that instance.[29] With equal clarity the law then states the effect of this abatement: it extinguishes the acts of the process.[30] Now, the instance is only a certain phase of the judicial process.[31] The decree of summons is but one act of the whole process. The fact that the summons is a procedural act does not thereby make it a part of the instance of the lawsuit. There is no difficulty, then, in saying that, whereas the abatement can occur only after the joinder of issue, it extinguishes *all* the acts of the process when it does occur, even those acts which preceded the joinder of issue. Hence, the term of computation for establishing the abatement of the instance will potentially begin from the joinder of issue, and not from the issuance of the summons.

Article 3. Persons Affected by the Abatement of the Instance

By provision of law the abatement of the instance comes into effect automatically. Its effects extend to all involved in the process, including those who are in their minority and those who are in law equivalent to minors. When necessary, an exception to further procedure as based on the abatement of the instance is to be raised even *ex officio* by the court itself. Those who are adversely affected by the abatement retain the right to sue their guardians, administrators, and proxies for damages suffered in consequence of the fault or negligence of these representatives.[32]

Datae, De Iudiciis pro Ecclesia Orientali Adnotationibus Fontium Auctae cura Pontificii Consilii Codici Iuris Canonici Orientalis Redigendo (Typis Polyglottis Vaticanis, 1950), Canon 254: Instantiae initium fit citatione . . . .

[28] Canon 1732: Instantiae initium fit litis contestatione . . . .

[29] Cf. canon 1736.

[30] Cf. canon 1738.

[31] Cf. *supra*, p. 42.

[32] Canon 1737: Peremptio obtinet ipso iure et adversus omnes, minores quoque aliosve minoribus aequiparatos, eaque ex officio etiam excipi debet, salvo iure regressus ad indemnitatem adversus tutores, administratores, procuratores qui culpa se caruisse non probaverint.

Although the abatement of the instance takes effect *ipso iure,* in practice its effects will not be operative until it is so declared by way of a judicial decree. All legitimate impediments forestalling procedural activity must be absent if the abatement is to take effect. Wherefore, in practice, the party desirous of a declaration of abatement requests such a declaration from the court. To ascertain the true state of affairs, the court then summons the parties for information regarding the reason for their inactivity before it decrees the abatement of the instance to be in effect.[83] No class of persons is exempt from the effects of the abatement. Persons in their minority and also those who in law are held equivalent to minors[84] are expressly included as subject to its effects. It should be noted, however, that the abatement of the instance cannot progress against the interests of such minors as are destitute of representation. In this latter event, not only would an interruption of the instance occur[85] and, hence, no abatement would be possible,[86] but the very factual situation alone would be enough to present a legitimate impediment to forestall the abatement.

Minors and those equivalently such may bring suit against those guardians or proxies through whose fault the abatement of the instance was allowed to occur. Such guardians, administrators, and proxies, therefore, are liable for whatever damages their charges suffer from the abatement unless they can prove absence of fault.

May an action seeking the restitution in law of their integral pristine position,[87] also be claimed? Coronata declares that it may be.[88] Vidal remarks with lesser conviction that the remedy indicated in the law, namely the action for damages against guardians, proxies, etc., does not seem to preclude the advantageous use of a *restitutio in integrum* as an extraordinary and more forceful rem-

[83] Wernz-Vidal, *De Processibus,* p. 374, n. 413.

[84] Cf. canon 100, § 3. Collegiate and non-collegiate moral persons are equivalent to minors.

[85] Cf. canon 1735.

[86] Cf. Coronata, *Institutiones,* III, p. 169, n. 1263.

[87] Cf. canon 1689.

[88] *Institutiones,* III, p. 169, n. 1263, footnote 3.

edy.[39] Lega-Bartoccetti say, on the other hand, that it seems certain that a *restitutio in integrum* may not be sought, since the express disposition of the law already concedes the right to bring suit for damages against negligent representatives. Moreover, Lega-Bartoccetti add, the very subject matter of the law, i.e., the abatement of the instance, precludes any restoration. Once extinguished, the instance cannot be resurrected. Since the instance and not the action is destroyed, however, the action may be brought in a new process and, hence, in a new instance. Therefore no substantial right is lost through the abatement of the previous instance.[40]

The writer readily admits the cogency of the argument presented by Lega-Bartoccetti. Admittedly, canon 1687 concedes to minors the extraordinary legal remedy of a *restitutio in integrum,* but it insists that this remedy is available to such as are seriously damaged by reason of a valid but rescissible act or concern. On two points, therefore, no application of the *restitutio in integrum* appears possible. First, no serious or permanent substantial right is necessarily debased, perverted or effaced through the abatement (in courts of a first hearing) since another hearing can always be instituted upon the same action. Secondly — and this seems the more important consideration — the abatement of the instance takes effect *ipso iure.* Hence, whatever be the damage that is suffered through the abatement, it does not emerge from a rescissible act or concern. It is only in the event that the instance in the appellate court is abated and, hence, that the issue would become irrevocably adjudged that the substantial rights of a litigant party would be gravely obstructed. Nevertheless, even if a *restitutio in integrum* could possibly be utilized, it would not resurrect the abated instance, but would rather allow the commencement of a new prosecution in the appellate court.

The weight of procedural practice in the Roman Rota, however, and specifically Article 84 of the *Normae* for the Rota, militate against the opinion here presented by the writer.[41] The norms of

[39] *De Processibus,* p. 374, n. 413.

[40] *Commentarius,* II, 586-587.

[41] *AAS,* XXVI (1934), 471.

Rotal procedure expressly permit the use of the *restitutio in integrum* when an abatement has occurred.[42] The weight of Rotal procedure, therefore, as a supplementary quide to canons 1905 and 1687 is too strong for much more that a theoretical opposite view relative to the sense and content of the law of the Code. In theory, therefore, and if juridical reasoning be limited solely to the contents of the Code of Canon Law, the present writer would deny the application of a *restitutio in integrum* whenever the abatement of the instance has occurred. In practice, however, the norm and example of the Roman Rota force him to admit the possibility of a *restitutio in integrum,* even in non-Rotal causes, though the abatement of the instance has occurred.[43]

How does the abatement of the instance become acknowledged? Litigant parties may propose the declaration of the abatement to the court either by way of a judicial exception or by way of a newly entered suit. Since the abatement is effected *ipso iure,* the litigant parties have the right to the effects of the law. This right, therefore, may be proposed either by way of a newly entered suit or by way of a judicial exception.[44] The judge, however, invokes the abatement only by way of a judicial exception.[45] The abatement of the instance is to be declared by the judge in whose court the abated instance had its rise or origin.[46]

Must the judge, however, always raise the exception of abate-

[42] Article 84: Ut causa quoquomodo finita iuxta art. 81 iterum in Rota tractari possit, pars, cuius interest, necesse est beneficium obtineat restitutionis in integrum adversus declaratam peremptionem, vel exspiratam Commissionem, a Supremo Tribunali Ap. Signaturae impetrandum; nisi agatur de causa iure proprio in prima instantia a S. Rota cognoscenda, quo in casu integrum est partibus causam iterum per novum libellum proponere.

The *restitutio in integrum* is however to be sought from the Apostolic Signatura, as is evident from the norm itself.

[43] As a guide for a norm of procedure the *stylus* and *praxis* of the Roman Curia are in canon 20 adverted to as applicable factors.

[44] Canon 1667: Quodlibet ius non solum actione munitur, nisi aliud expresse cautum sit, sed etiam exceptione, quae semper competit et est suapte natura perpetua.

[45] Cf. canon 1618, where the general rule is stated by which the interest of the court is to be regulated: *In negotio quod privatorum solummodo interest, iudex procedere potest dumtaxat ad instantiam partis. . . .*

[46] Coronata, *Institutiones,* III, p. 168, n. 1263.

ment whenever it is applicable? Coronata maintains[47] that the exception of abatement must be raised only in those proceedings in which the promoter of justice or the defender of the bond are involved. Evidently, for his argument, the norm of canon 1618 overshadows and supplants the express words of canon 1737.[48] To this argument one must object that the abatement of the instance is intended as an institute of law for the good order of procedure, and hence for the public good whereby the rights of private individuals are the better defended.[49] Moreover, the law expressly states that the exception of the abatement must be raised even *ex officio*. Accordingly, it is the opinion of the writer that the judge must always invoke the exception of abatement whenever it is applicable.

By force of the very same argument, i.e., since the abatement takes effect *ipso iure* and since it is fundamentally constituted for the public good, the litigant parties cannot by accord renounce the abatement of the instance.[51]

Article 4. The Effects of the Abatement of the Instance

The abatement of the instance extinguishes the acts of the process which concern the form of procedure, but not the acts of the cause which bear on the merits of the issue itself. The acts which bear on the merits of the issue retain their juridical value even for another prosecution provided that the same persons and the same object of controversy are involved in the proceedings of the new lawsuit. As far as third persons are concerned, these acts on the merits of the cause have only documentary force.[52]

[47] *Op. cit.*, III, p. 169, n. 1263.

[48] Canon 1737: . . . ex officio etiam excipi debet . . . .

[49] Cf. Lega-Bartoccetti, *Commentarius*, II, 586.

states that the abatement of the instance is effected *ipso iure*,[50] and

[50] Canon 1737: Peremptio obtinet ipso iure . . . .

[51] Cf. Roberti, *De Processibus*, II, p. 11, n. 315; for the contrary opinion cf. Coronata, *Institutiones*, III, p. 168, n. 1263, and p. 169, n. 1263, footnote 1.

[52] Canon 1738: Peremptio extinquit acta processus, non vero acta causae; imo haec vim habere possunt etiam in alia instantia, dummodo ea inter easdem personas et super eadem re intercedat; sed ad extraneos quod attinet, non aliam vim obtinent, nisi documentorum.

Canon 1642, § 1, defines the judicial acts which bear on the merits of the issue in the cause as *acta causae*. These acts are the decisions that have been given, and the proofs of every kind that have been submitted. The same canon defines procedural acts (*acta processus*) as the acts which are concerned with the formalities of procedure, e.g., the summonses, the presentation of the *libellus*, etc. Thus, by canon 1738, the acts that bear on the merits of the cause remain of juridical value even after the abatement of the instance. It is altogether congruous that the proofs already established be retained; there is no reason why proofs in one set of proceedings should become valueless in a second or new period of prosecution in the trial. If they establish proof earlier, then they should retain possession of their probative value also later for any successive prosecution period in a trial.[53]

The abatement of the instance does not effect the legal prescription of the action or the suit. The right of action remains and may be proposed anew. Accordingly, the new prosecution is begun and proceeds as though the abated instance had not run its course, except for the fact that the existing acts which bear on the merits of the issue in the cause are retained in full juridic force so long as the matter rests on the same issue and between the same litigant parties.[54]

It is quite just that the decisions, proofs, and all acts whatsoever that throw light on the merits of the cause be made applicable only to the same litigant parties and to the same object of litigation that was involved in the previous abated instance. When a new object of litigation arises between the same litigant parties, it seems that the proofs of the previously abated instance retain only the probative force of documents in the new cause.[55]

All that is accomplished in a trial is subject to the examination and eventual contradiction of the litigant parties. Decisions in the cause may not be pronounced if they are based solely on the allegations and deposition of one of the litigant parties. Each litigant

[53] Roberti, *De Processibus*, II, p. 12, n. 315.

[54] Cf. Wernz-Vidal, *De Processibus*, p. 375, n. 414.

[55] For this deduction cf. canon 1738 in conjunction with canon 20 as a guide for procedure.

must have the opportunity to defend himself against the allegations and deposition of his opponent. Hence, the juridical force of the *acta causae* in another set of proceedings is retained only when the same litigant parties are involved. A third party in a new process would be at an unfair advantage or disadvantage in respect to his opponent were he to benefit from the full probative value of a preceding instance without himself having been a contesting party in that instance. Only the original parties involved should benefit or suffer detriment from what has already been executed in a judicial process between them.[56]

The *acta causae* of an abated instance, however, retain some force in a judicial process when a new litigant or a third contestant party is involved. The law declares such acts to have the force of documents in this event.[57] Therefore, some presumption of truth must be given them when they are applicable, even in causes involving other litigant parties and other litigated issues.[58] It seems that these acts are presumed true by a simple presumption of law.[59]

One may raise a question regarding the effect of the abatement of the instance upon interlocutory sentences, i.e., decisions upon incidental issues in the trial. The norm of canon 1738 is equally applicable to them. If the interlocutory (incidental) decisions bear on the merits of the cause, they fully retain their juridical value in a succeeding prosecution when the same litigant parties and the same litigated issues are involved, but have documentary force

[56] Cf. Regula 22, *R. J.* in VI°: "Non debet aliquis alterius odio praegravari." For an explanation of the scope of this rule of law, cf. Bartoccetti, *De Regulis Juris Canonici* (Roma: Belardetti, 1955) pp. 104-106.

[57] Cf. canon 1738: . . . sed ad extraneos quod attinet, non aliam vim obtineat, nisi documentorum.

[58] Canons 1816 and 1817 state what juridic force documents have.

Canon 1816: Documenta publica fidem faciunt de iis quae directe et principaliter in eisdem affirmantur.

Canon 1817: Documentum privatum, sive agnitum a parte sive recognitum a iudice, probat adversus auctorem vel subscriptorem et causam ab eis habentes, perinde ac confessio extra iudicium facta; sed per se non habet vim probandi adversus extraneos.

[59] Coronata, *Institutiones*, III, p. 170, n. 1264, footnote 1.

only, when new litigants or different issues are concerned. Interlocutory sentences concerned purely with procedural formalities are extinguished as are all other *acta processus*. This solution offers no difficulty when the abatement occurs in the court of first hearing. The problem appears when the abatement of the instance occurs in the appellate court.

Canon 1736 states the general rule that an abated instance in the appellate court results in the establishment of the appealed sentence as a *res iudicata,* i.e., as irrevocably adjudicated. When this abatement of the instance occurs in the appellate court, what becomes of the value of the interlocutory decisions regarding the merits of the cause which are declared in the appellate court? Indeed, such interlocutory decisions in the appellate court may tend to weaken or destroy the very basis upon which rests the sentence that is being tried on appeal. Do these interlocutory decisions, however, suffice to prevent the passing of the appealed sentence into a *res iudicata* when an abatement of the instance in the appellate court occurs? Lega-Bartoccetti assert that an abated instance in the court of appeal will not effect a *res iudicata* for the sentence on appeal when the interlocutory decisions which bear on the merits of the cause are established in this appellate court.[60] It is claimed that such interlocutory decisions suffice to destroy the foundation upon which rests the decision of the court of first hearing. Consequently it is argued that the appealed sentence cannot attain the force of a *res iudicata,* since it cannot itself be considered as then having any authoritative force.[61] Does canon 1738, then, implicitly establish an exception to the rule, enunciated in canon 1736, which states that an abated instance in the appellate court will result in a *res iudicata* of the sentence on appeal? Lega-Bartoccetti answer in the affirmative.[62] To this the writer cannot agree. When the law does not distinguish then no distinction seems in place.[63] Canon 1726 makes no distinction. It clearly states

[60] *Commentarius,* II, 590-593.

[61] *Op. cit.,* II, 592.

[62] *Loc. cit.*

[63] "Ubi lex non distinguit nec nos distinguere debemus." A canonical adage drawn from D. (32, 25): "Cum in verbis nulla ambiguitas est, non debet admitti voluntatis quaestio."

that an appealed sentence becomes irrevocably adjudicated whenever the abated instance occurs in the appellate court.[64]

It is true that the consequences of the abatement of the instance in the appellate court are more serious than those of abatement in the court of first hearing. A *res iudicata* cannot be impugned directly and can be invoked to prevent a new introduction of the same cause.[65] Nevertheless, it must be remembered that the abatement of the instance is not an arbitrary affair. Sufficient safeguards to prevent its occurrence are given in the law itself.[66] The very purpose of abatement establishes it as an institute for the public good, for a good procedural order whereby the rights of individuals may be better preserved. It is constituted by law to prevent interminable and unwieldy litigation while at the same time allowing for the proper presentation of the litigated issue.[67] Hence, the culpable negligence of a litigant party to prevent the abatement of the instance deserves no condonation. The consequences resulting to his detriment are attributable to his own fault.[68] The opposing litigant should not be penalized in those benefits which the law itself establishes. Indeed, the abatement of the instance is equivalent to a tacit renunciation of that instance. Hence, the consequences attendant upon the abatement of the instance are but a natural sequel tacitly acknowledged and accepted by the litigant parties. Otherwise, the resolution of such causes could become interminable. The very purpose of the institute of the *peremptio instantiae* would thus be nullified. This writer believes, therefore, that an abated instance in the appellate court will result in a *res iudicata* of the sentence on appeal, notwithstanding the interlocutory decisions on the merits of the cause which may have been declared in that appellate court.

A question may also arise regarding the possible effect of the abatement of the instance upon the computation of the time neces-

[64] Cf. canon 1736: . . . in gradu appellationis . . . sententia per appellationem oppugnata transit in rem iudicatam.

[65] Cf. canon 1904.

[66] Cf. canon 1736.

[67] Lega-Bartoccetti, *Commentarius*, II, 586.

[68] *Reg. 25, R. J.*, in VI°: "Mora sua cuilibet est nociva."

sary for the legal prescription of an action or suit. Canon 1725, 4°, declares that a judicial summons interrupts the computation of the time necessary for an operative legal prescription. It may be asked, then, whether the abatement of the instance cancels out this interruption so that a legal prescription of the action or suit may run its course. It is the opinion of the writer that the abatement of the instance will extinguish the interruption occasioned for the legal prescription of an action or suit by the judicial summons. Of course, the question here centers upon the abatement in courts of first hearing; the abatement in courts of appeal effects a *res iudicata* of the sentence already established in the court of first hearing. The abatement of the instance extinguishes the process and the juridical effects of that process.[69] With the extinction of the summons as a procedural act, the juridical obstacle preventing the legal prescription of an action or suit is removed. Hence, the legal prescription of the action or suit may now continue to run its course.[70]

As to the expenses incurred in consequence of the abatement of the instance, each litigant bears the expenses which accrue from the judicial acts attributable to him in the abated instance.[71] It seems to the writer, however, that the expenses incurred in consequence of the abatement of the instance in a court of appeal should be attributable to him who instituted the appeal. With the abatement of the instance in a court of appeal the resultant irrevocable decision[72] concludes the matter of controversy. The litigant party who instituted the appeal thereby loses his suit, and the party who loses the suit must as a rule repay to the winner the court costs.[73]

[69] Cf. canon 1738; Lega-Bartoccetti, *Commentarius*, II, 590, footnote 1.

[70] The other effects listed in canon 1725 are likewise modified by the extinction of the summons as a procedural act.

[71] Canon 1739: In casu peremptionis, quas quisque ex litigatoribus fecerit, has ipse ferat expensas perempti iudicii.

[72] Cf. canon 1736, *ad finem*.

[73] Cf. canon 1910.

CHAPTER VII

THE RENUNCIATION OF THE INSTANCE AND OF THE ACTS OF THE PROCESS

Article 1. The Notion and Object of the Renunciation of the Instance and of the Acts of the Process

The renunciation of the instance occurs when the plaintiff declares in juridical form that he wishes the process closed without further progress.[1] The renunciation of the instance, therefore, derives from the express will of the plaintiff, in which at least implicitly the defendant concurs, whereas the abatement of the instance occurs as a tacit renunciation to further procedure by both litigant parties. The renunciation of the instance, moreover, must be clearly distinguished from the renunciation of the action itself and from the renunciation of some of the acts of the judicial process. Even though the instance of the lawsuit be renounced, the right to bring action on the same issue in controversy does not thereby become extinct. The action may be proposed in a new prosecution, unless of course indirectly the action itself has been juridically lost, e.g., when the instance is renounced in the appellate court and thereby the sentence on appeal become a *res iudicata.*

The renunciation of the right to action is not the concern of this commentary. The right of action itself may be renounced or abandoned at any time, and through such a renunciation not only the action but, as is evident, the prosecution itself and all the judicial acts of the trial are concomitantly renounced.[2] The concern of this commentary rests with the renunciation of the instance itself and with the renunciation of one or some of the procedural acts in the judicial process. Herein also a distinction must be made. The renunciation of one or some of the acts of the process is not the

[1] Roberti, *De Processibus,* II, pp. 13-14, n. 318.

[2] Cf. Coronata, *Institutiones,* III, p. 170, n. 1265.

same as the renunciation of the instance itself. The renunciation of one or some of the acts of the process affects only those specific acts which are renounced without prejudice to the remaining acts or to the continued prosecution itself.

The plaintiff may renounce the instance of a lawsuit at any stage of the trial and in any jurisdictional sequence of it, e.g., in the court of first hearing, or in the court of appeal. In like manner, both the plaintiff and the defendant may renounce some or all of the acts of the process.[3]

The express renunciation of the instance produces the same effect as does the abatement of the instance, which abatement is a tacit renunciation of the instance.[4] Canon 1741 expressly states that an admitted renunciation has for the renounced acts the same effect as the abatement of the instance. Hence, in the renunciation of the instance or of some of its acts, only the acts of the process and not the acts bearing on the merits of the cause (*acta causae*) are the concern of this canon. The renunciation of the *acta causae* as such is not considered in this canon.

Noval, however, in speaking of the individual acts which can be renounced, claims that the renunciation of the *acta causae* is also contemplated in this canon.[5] It must be admitted that a relatively recent decision from the Commission for the Authentic Interpretation of the Code with regard to canon 1890[6] does not regard the difference of terminology between the *acta processus* and the *acta*

[3] Canon 1740, § 1: In quolibet statu et gradu iudicii potest actor instantiae renuntiare; item tum actor tum reus possunt processus actis renuntiare sive omnibus sive nonnullis tantum.

[4] Canon 1741: Admissa, pro actis quibus renuntiatum est, eosdem parit effectus ac peremptio instantiae . . . ;

[5] *De Iudiciis*, n. 428; cf. also Blat, *Commentarium Textus Codicis Iuris Canonici* (6 vols., Lib. IV, *De Processibus*, Romae: Collegio Angelico, 1927), p. 259, n. 238; Vermeersch-Creusen, *Epitome Iuris Canonici*, III, p. 71, n. 155. Vidal (*De Processibus*, p. 375, n. 415) seems to hold the same position: "Renuntians debet solvere expensas actuum, quibus renuntiavit, *qui inde carent valore iuridico nec a iudice aestimandi sunt in sententia proferenda.*"

[6] Cf. Bouscaren, *Canon Law Digest*, II, 469. The Code Commission was asked: Whether the words *acta causae*, in canon 1890, refer to all the judicial records. Reply: In the affirmative. Cf. *AAS*, XXXIV (1942), 50.

causae[7] as consistent throughout the Code. Hence, the argument that the *acta causae* are also included within the scope of canons 1740-1741 may at first glance appear valid. Both the text, however, and the context of the law make clear the object of the renunciation.[8] Canon 1740, § 1, deals directly with the renunciation of the instance and with the renunciation of all or some of the acts of the process (*acta processus*). Moreover, canon 1741 clearly states that this renunciation gives rise to the same effects as does the abatement of the instance. Canon 1738 leaves no further room for doubt, for it states that the abatement of the instance extinguishes the acts of the process (*acta processus*), but not the acts that bear on the merits of the cause (*acta causae*).[9] The law here does not deal with the renunciation of the action, nor with the acts that bear on the merits of the cause. The renunciation of the *acta causae* has no need of the conditions established by law under these canons (cc. 1740-1741). They may be renounced[10] by the litigant party whose interests they serve, even when the trial does not pend.[11]

Canon 1740, § 1, treats of the renunciation of the instance by the plaintiff. The same canon then treats of the renunciation of some or of all of the acts of the process by both the plaintiff and the defendant. The question thereupon arises: why does canon 1740, § 1, treat only of the plaintiff when it states that he can renounce the instance, and then, in the next clause, treat of both the plaintiff and the defendant when it states that they may renounce

[7] Cf. canon 1642, § 1.

[8] Cf. canon 18, according to which the first rule for doctrinal interpretation derives from the proper signification of the words of the law taken in their text and context. Only thereafter, if some doubt remain, should one have recourse to parallel places, if there are any, to the purpose and the circumstances of the law, and to the mind of the legislator himself.

[9] Canon 1738: Peremptio exstinguit acta processus, non vero acta causae. . . .

[10] Provided the adverse party does not object, Cf., e.g., canon 1759, § 4.

[11] Lega-Bartoccetti, *Commentarius,* II, 597: "Res est autem in canone de *actis processus* et non de *actis causae* quia instantia coalescit, per se, ex actis processus et non ex actis causae, quae cum non perimantur perempta instantia, exinde possunt renunciari etiam non pendente iudicio et horum renunciatio non indiget iis conditionibus in canone significatis quae pertinent ad ipsam rationem processus."

some or all of the acts of the process? The reading of the law seems to make a distinction between the renunciation of the instance and the renunciation of all of the acts of the process. Otherwise, why is the renunciation of the instance apparently limited to the plaintiff, and why then follows the open assertion that both the plaintiff and the defendant may renounce all the acts of the process? Does the law distinguish the acts of the process when renounced through the renunciation of the instance from the sum total of all of the acts of the process? Since all the acts of the process are canceled out through the renunciation of the instance, can there be a distinction between the renunciation of the instance and the renunciation of all of the acts of the process?

Roberti states that the renunciation of all of the acts of the process resolves itself into the renunciation of the instance itself, if we except the case in which there is a renunciation of all those acts of the process that preceded the joinder of issue.[12] Previous to the joinder of issue the instance does not yet formally exist. Vidal remarked that apart from renouncing the instance, either of the litigant parties or both of them can renounce some or all of the acts of the process.[13]

Lega-Bartoccetti offer a simple solution. The express reading of the canon gives one aspect only, that of the renunciation of the instance as coming from one party alone, although both litigant parties, so Lega-Bartoccetti contend, can renounce the instance.[14] For the renunciation to take effect the mutual consent of the opposing litigants is required.[15] The acceptance of the adverse litigant's renunciation is thus also a species of renunciation.[16]

[12] *De Processibus,* II, p. 16, n. 317.

[13] *De Processibus,* p. 375, n. 415.

[14] *Commentarius,* II, 598.

[15] Cf. canon 1740,§ 2; cf. however, *Norm. S.R.R.*, Art. 89, § 2—*AAS,* XXVI (1934), 471, and Pinna, *Praxis Iudicialis,* p. 52, where it is stated that the renunciation can be admitted by the judge in causes which respect the public good, even though the adverse party opposes it, provided, however, that the promoter of justice or the defender of the bond is consulted on the matter.

[16] Lega-Bartoccetti, *loc. cit.*

This solution of the problem regarding the efficient cause of the renunciation may seem dubious if one considers the ridiculous circumstance of a defendant presuming to renounce acts of the process which tend to be detrimental to himself. The argument is substantially sound, however, since the law evidently understands that neither will the defendant undertake to execute such a rash folly nor will the plaintiff acquiesce in such a renunciation. Hence, for all practical purposes, each litigant party will be able to renounce only those acts of the process undertaken in the advancement of his own interests and without objection from his opponent. Since the plaintiff has usually the most to lose by renouncing the instance, inasmuch as the judicial process was started on his initiative, it is but natural that the law should treat of the plaintiff alone as renouncing the instance. Thus, the apparent limiting of the renunciation of the instance to the plaintiff and the ensuing confusion as to the possible distinction of the effects of the renunciation of the instance from those of the renunciation of all of the acts of the process may be resolved.

This solution appears the only plausible one to the present writer. An alternate possible solution would be that the law's reference to the ability of either the plaintiff or the defendant to renounce all of the acts of the process applies only in those causes wherein the judicial process has not yet progressed to the joinder of issue (*litis contestatio*). In this explanation a distinction between all of the acts of the process therein renounced (as far as the joinder of issue) and the effects of the renunciation of the instance (which does not exist before the joinder of issue) would be valid. It must be added, however, that this latter explanation appears less satisfying, since the law itself makes no such distinction.

The renunciation of the instance or of some or of all of the procedural acts may be made at any stage of the trial.[17] In a technical sense, however, the instance of the lawsuit cannot be renounced prior to the joinder of issue, since the instance of the lawsuit does not yet exist at that point. Since all or some of the procedural acts

[17] Canon 1740, § 1.

may also be renounced at any stage of the trial, the acts of the process preceding the joinder of issue may be renounced.[18]

The renunciation of the instance or of some of the procedural acts may be made at any jurisdictional sequence in the trial. As in the abatement of the instance, so in its renunciation, the acts of the process are extinguished, and not the action itself. But when the instance of the appellate court is renounced, the sentence on appeal becomes a *res iudicata,* indirectly thereby surrendering the action itself.[19]

Article 2. The Formalities to be Observed in the Renunciation

To be valid, the renunciation of the instance or of the acts of the process must be made in writing; it must be signed by the party making the renunciation, or by the proxy who has been endowed with this right by a special mandate from the litigant party whom he represents; it must be submitted to the other litigant party and accepted or at least not opposed by him; and it must be admitted or allowed by the judge.[20]

[18] Cf. Coronata, *Institutiones,* III, p. 170, n. 1265, for an opposite opinion. Coronata says that no renunciation either of the instance or of the acts of the process may be made before the joinder of issue, nor may any renunciation be made after the principal sentence in the cause has been given. The *Normae S. R. R.,* Art. 84 — *AAS,* XXVI (1934), 471 — however admit the renunciation of a bill of complaint before the joinder of issue even apart from a consulting of the defendant. The *Normae S. R. R.,* moreover, treat of the renunciation of the instance when this renunciation is made after the *sententia* in the cause has been reached. Cf. Article 90:

§ 1. Si actor, introducta causa in prima instantia in S. Rota, ante alterius partis citationem renuntiet libello iam oblato, Ponens renuntiationem admittet altera parte inaudita, audito tamen Promotore iustitiae, vel vinculi Defensore, in causis quae bonum publicum salutemve animarum respiciant.

§ 2. Renuntiatio instantiae, facta post sententiae prolationem a parte victa, aequivalet rei iudicatae irrevocabili contra renuntiantem. — *AAS,* XXVI (1934), 473.

[19] Cf. Lega-Bartoccetti, *Commentarius, II,* 598.

[20] Canon 1740, § 2: Renuntiatio ut valeat, peragenda est in scriptis, et a parte vel ab eius procuratore, speciali tamen mandato munito, debet subscribi, alteri parti communicari, ab eaque acceptari. vel saltem non impugnari, et a iudice admitti.

An accepted written renunciation becomes an *actus causae,* since it concerns a decision affecting the cause inasmuch as it gives proof of a valid renunciation which may be called upon in a further instance. Whether this renunciation is made in the judicial forum itself or extrajudicially, its juridical value will be the same, provided the juridical fact of its establishment can be ascertained.[21] The written document of the renunciation, therefore, must be signed by the party instituting the renunciation. It must be accepted at least tacitly by the adverse litigant in a form which establishes this acceptance as a juridical fact capable of proof.[22] Finally, the renunciation must be admitted by the court. In admitting the renunciation, the judge issues a decree to that effect and notifies all those who are involved in the cause.[23]

In practice, the written renunciation of the instance or of some of the acts of the process is signed by the party making the renunciation, and is directed to the judge, who then communicates a copy of this statement to the other litigant party, allowing this other party a sufficient interval of time to decide whether he may wish to oppose the renunciation. After the expiration of this interval for deliberation, or when the adverse party forthwith accepts the renunciation, the judge issues a decree in which he establishes the effective renunciation as a juridical fact.[24]

In contrast to the pre-Code law, which required that the renunciation of the instance be made in simple fashion and free of all conditions,[25] the law today does not require the renunciation to be made so absolutely.[26] In matters involving the interests of private individuals alone, the judge should always permit the renunciation of the instance or of some of the acts of the process. In matters in-

[21] Lega-Bartoccetti, *Commentarius,* II, 598.

[22] Cf. *Normae S. R. R.,* Article 89, § 2, and 90, § 1 — *AAS,* XXVI (1934), 472-473 — which, however, allow the renunciation even though opposed by the adverse party in matters of the public good, and permit also the renunciation of the *libellus,* even before the summons to the adverse party is issued.

[23] Pinna, *Praxis Iudicialis,* p. 52.

[24] Wernz-Vidal, *De Processibus,* p. 375, n. 415.

[25] Cf. *Regolamento Legislativo,* § 912.

[26] Cf. Roberti, *De Processibus,* II, p. 14, n. 316; Coronata, *Institutiones,* III, p. 171, n. 1265; Lega-Bartoccetti, *Commentarius,* II, 598, footnote 1.

volving the public welfare, the promoter of justice (in marriage causes, also the defender of the bond) can be called to prosecute the instance of the lawsuit, notwithstanding the withdrawal of an individual litigant party.[27]

Guardians, administrators, and such as act for moral persons seem not to need any special permission to renounce some of the acts of the process which do not exceed the importance of matters within their ordinary administration. The same is true for the renunciation of the instance in the lower courts, i.e., in the courts of first hearing.[28] The renunciation of the instance in the appellate court, however, would involve an irrevocable sentence. Such a renunciation of the instance in the appellate court could seriously and permanently damage the interests of those for whom these guardians and administrators act. Such a renunciation, therefore, may be considered beyond the limits of ordinary administration since the right of action itself may thus be indirectly lost.[29] Hence, guardians and those who act as administrators for moral personalities may not renounce the instance of an appellate court without the consent of those whom they represent.[30] The requisite permission for the guardians of insane persons or of infants to renounce the instance or to renounce any acts of the process which exceed matters of ordinary administration seems to pertain to the ordinary or the judge.[31]

Proxies, however, need a special mandate to effect the renunciation of the instance or of any of the procedural acts, i.e., either to propose such a renunciation or to accept it.[32] The pronouncement of law on this matter is explicit.[33] Hence, unless they be given

[27] Roberti, *De Processibus*, II, p. 15, n. 316.

[28] Roberti, *loc. cit.*

[29] Lega-Bartoccetti, *Commentarius*, II, 599.

[30] Cf. Coronata, *Institutiones*, III, p. 171, n. 1266.

[31] Cf. canon 1648, § 1, and especially canon 1652, on whose provisions a safe norm of procedure in this matter can be based.

[32] Cf. canon 1740, § 2, and canon 1662.

[33] Canon 1740, § 2: Renuntiatio ut valeat, peragenda est in scriptis, et a parte *vel ab eius procuratore, speciali tamen mandato munito,* debet subscribi . . . .

Canon 1662: *Nisi speciale mandatum habuerit,* procurator non potest renuntiare actioni. instantiae vel actis iudicialibus . . . . (Italics supplied by the writer).

special permission by their principals to do so, proxies may not renounce the instance or any of the acts of the process.

Article 3. The Effects of the Renunciation

A valid renunciation produces the same effects as those which are caused by the abatement of the instance. The one instituting the renunciation, however, is alone liable for the judicial expenses or costs of the acts which he renounced.[34] The acts of the process, therefore, and not the acts bearing on the merits of the cause (*acta causae*), are extinguished. When the instance itself is renounced, the *acta causae* retain their probative value in any later prosecution of the lawsuit, provided the litigated issue is presented by the same litigant parties and regarding the same matter.[35] When different litigants or third persons are concerned, these *acta causae* have the force of documents only.[36] When the instance of the appellate court is renounced, there are produced the same effects that follow from the abatement of the instance, namely, the issue in litigation as decided in the first instance becomes a *res iudicata.* A valid renunciation cannot later be rejected by the litigant parties, since the effect of the renunciation becomes sustained by the law itself.[37] As in the abatement of the instance so through the renunciation of the instance there is canceled out whatever interruption would prevent the running of its course on the part of the legal prescription of an action or suit.[38]

The incurred liability for judicial expenses in a renounced instance or for any renounced acts differs, however, from the incurred obligations that arise through an abated instance. The judicial expenses incurred in consequence of a renunciation, whether of the instance or of any of the procedural acts, devolve upon that

[34] Canon 1741: Admissa, pro actis quibus renuntiatum est, eosdem parit effectus ac peremptio instantiae; et obligat renuntiantem ad solvendas expensas actorum, quibus renuntiatum fuit.

[35] Cf. canon 1738.

[36] *Loc. cit.*

[37] Cf. canon 1741 in conjunction with canon 1737; Regula 21, *R. J.*, in VI°: "Quod semel placuit amplius displicere non potest"; Lega-Bartoccetti, *Commentarius,* II, 602, footnote 1.

[38] Cf. *supra,* pp. 89-90.

litigant party who institutes the renunciation. If the litigant party renounces only one or some of the procedural acts, he is liable for only those acts.[39] The judicial expenses incurred in consequence of the abatement of an instance, on the other hand, are shared by both litigant parties, in such a way, however, that each is liable for only those acts which he responsibly introduced in the judicial process.[40]

Since canon 1741 itself obliges the party initiating the renunciation to bear the judicial expenses deriving therefrom, no sentence of condemnation for judicial expenses needs be issued by the court. Such expenses are owed by the renouncing litigant in view of the law's own specific provision.[41]

The renunciation of the instance is akin to the abatement of the instance. Whereas the former is an express renunciation, the latter (the abatement of the instance) is a tacit renunciation. The effects produced by both are the same, with the exception already noted in the matter of judicial expenses.

One final word of contrast may be noted between the two. The abatement of the instance is indivisible in the sense that, whenever it occurs, its effects are incumbent upon all who are concerned in the process.[42] The effect of the renunciation of the instance, on the other hand, is divisible in the sense that, when several plaintiffs or defendants in their own right are present in the process, the renunciation of the instance by one or the other of the litigants will not prejudice the continuance of that instance, i.e., the prosecution of the trial, by the remaining litigants.[43]

[39] Cf. canon 1741.
[40] Cf. canon 1739.
[41] Cf. Lega-Bartoccetti, *Commentarius,* II, 602.
[42] Roberti, *De Processibus,* II, p. 10, n. 313.
[43] *Ibid.*, p. 14, n. 316.

CONCLUSIONS

1. The *litis instantia* and the *peremptio instantiae* are fundamentally institutes of Roman law.

2. The concept of the *litis instantia* is not synonymous with that of *iudicium* or *processus*. The *litis instantia* properly refers to the judicial contention between the litigant parties which occurs in that part of the judicial process that begins from the joinder of issue (*litis contestatio*) and comprises the many judiciary acts which culminate in the rendering of the judicial decision (*sententia*).

3. An irrevocable sentence (*res iudicata*) is not necessary for concluding the *litis instantia*. The *litis instantia* will end with a definitive sentence in the cause and in whatever other way the proceedings of the trial are brought to a close.

4. Simple excommunication, i.e., excommunication not declared by way of a declaratory or inflicted by means of a condemnatory sentence, does not change the juridical status of the principal litigants in the trial.

5. Canon 1735, which treats of the interruption of the *litis instantia* on the part of proxies and guardians, does not establish a norm of procedure different from the norm enacted in canon 1733, which treats of the interruption of the *instantia* on the part of the principal litigants.

6. Since the abatement of the proceedings (*peremptio instantiae*) is effected *ipso iure,* the judge must *ex officio* raise the exception of abatement whenever it is applicable. The litigant parties cannot by accord renounce the abatement of the proceedings. It is only from the moment of the effected joinder of issue that the term of computation for the abatement of the proceedings will be reckoned.

7. An abated *instantia* in the appellate court will result in a *res iudicata* of the sentence on appeal notwithstanding any inter-

locutory decision on the merits of the issue in the cause which may have been declared in that appellate court. Rotal practice permits for grave and just reasons a *restitutio in integrum* when the abatement of the proceedings has occurred. The law of the Code in itself, however, does not seem to permit this extraordinary remedy.

8. The abatement of the proceedings removes the juridic obstacle which interrupted the course of legal prescription relative to the action or suit. In like manner, the renunciation of the proceedings will permit the continued progress of legal prescription relative to the action or suit.

9. As in the abatement of the proceedings (which is a tacit renunciation of the proceedings) so the renunciation of the proceedings affects only the acts of the process (*acta processus*), which are concerned with the formalities of procedure, and not those acts which bear on the merits of the issue(*acta causae*). The renunciation of the proceedings becomes an *actus causae,* since it is concerned with a decision which may be called upon in respect to the merits of the issue in a further instance or prosecution.

10. In effect, both litigant parties establish the renunciation of the proceedings (*renuntiatio instantiae*). Acts of the process which are concerned with matters not exceeding the importance of ordinary administration may be renounced by guardians and by administrators. All proxies, however, need a special mandate for renunciation, i.e., either to propose or to accept a renunciation.

11. The renunciation of all of the acts of the process after the joinder of issue is equivalent to the renunciation of the proceedings (*renuntiatio instantiae*).

The renunciation of all of the acts of the process previous to the joinder of issue is, in a technical sense, not the same as the renunciation of the instance, since the *instantia* of the lawsuit does not yet exist.

BIBLIOGRAPHY

SOURCES

Acta Apostolicae Sedis, Commentarium Officiale, Romae, 1909 —

Bouscaren, T. Lincoln, *The Canon Law Digest,* 3 vols. and Supplements (Bouscaren-O'Connor) through 1955, Milwaukee, Wis.: The Bruce Publishing Co., 1934, 1943, 1954, 1955, 1956.

Canones et Decreta Sacrosancti et Oecumenici Concilii Tridentini, Paulo III, Julio III, et Pio IV, Parisiis, 1754.

Codex Iuris Canonici Pii X Pontificis Maximi iussu digestus, Benedicti Papae XV auctoritate promulgatus, Praefatione, Fontium Annotatione et Indice Analytico-Alphabetico ab Emö Petro Card. Gasparri Auctus, Romae: Typis Polyglottis Vaticanis, 1917; reimpressio, 1934.

Codex Theodosianus, ed. P. Krueger, Berolini: Apud Weidmannos, 1923-1926.

Codicis Iuris Canonici Fontes, cura Emí Petri Card. Gasparri editi, 9 vols., Romae (postea Civitate Vaticana): Typis Polyglottis Vaticanis, 1923-1939 (Vols. VII-IX, ed. cura et studio Emï Iustiniani Card. Serédi).

Corpus Iuris Canonici, ed. Lipsiensis secunda, post Aemilii Richteri curas . . . instruxit Aemilius Friedberg, 2 vols., Lipsiae, 1879-1881.

Corpus Iuris Civilis, 3 vols., Berolini: Apud Weidmannos, 1928-1929; Vol. I, *Institutiones,* ed. stereotypa quinta decima, quas recognovit P. Krueger; *Digesta,* quae recognovit T. Mommsen et retractavit P. Krueger; Vol. II, *Codex Iustinianus,* ed. stereotypa decima, recognovit et retractavit P. Krueger; Vol. III, *Novellae,* ed. stereotypa quinta, quas recognovit R. Schoell et absolvit G. Kroll.

Decisiones Sacrae Romanae Rotae coram R.P.D. Marcello Crescentio, 5 vols., Romae, 1754.

Decretales D. Gregorii Papae IX, suae integritati una cum glossis restitutae, cum privilegio Gregorii XIII, Pont. Max., et Aliorum Principum, Romae, 1582.

Gaius, *Institutiones,* ed. Johannes Baviera, in *Fontes Iuris Romani Antejustiniani,* Florentiae, 1909.

Haenel, Gustavus, *Lex Romana Visigothorum,* Berolini, 1849.

Liber Sextus Decretalium D. Bonifacii Papae VIII, suae integritati cum Clementinis et Extravagantibus, earumque Glossis restitutis, Romae, 1582.

Litterae Apostolicae Motu Proprio Datae, De Iudiciis pro Ecclesia Orientali, Adnotationibus Fontium Auctae cura Pontificii Consilii Codici Iuris Canonici Orientalis Redigendo, Typis Polyglottis Vaticanis, 1950.

New Testament of Our Lord Jesus Christ, The, Confraternity Edition, Paterson, New Jersey: Saint Anthony's Guild Press, 1941.

Regolamento Legislativo e Giudiziario per gli Affari Civili emanato dalla Santità di Nostro Signore Gregorio Papa XVI con Moto Proprio del 10 Novembre, 1834, Romae: dalla Tipografia Camerale, 1834.

Sacrae Romanae Rotae Decisiones seu Sententiae (*ab anno 1909*), Romae: Typis Vaticanis, 1921 - -

Schroeder, H. J., *Canons and Decrees of the Council of Trent,* Saint Louis: B. Herder Book Company, 1941.

Theodosiani Libri XVI cum Constitutionibus Sirmondianis; ediderunt T. Mommsen et P. M. Meyer, adsumpto apparatu P. Krueger, 3 vols., Berolini, 1905.

REFERENCE WORKS

Augustine, Charles, *A Commentary on the New Code of Canon Law,* 8 vols., Saint Louis: Herder and Co., Vol. VII, 2. ed., 1925.

Barbosa, Augustinus, *Collectanea Doctorum tam Veterum quam Recentiorum, in Ius Pontificium Universum,* Lugduni, 1656.

Bartoccetti, V., *De Regulis Juris Canonici,* Roma: A. Belardetti, 1955.

Beste, Udalricus, *Introductio in Codicem,* 3 ed., Collegeville, Minn.: Saint John's Abbey Press, 1946.

Blat, Alberto, *Commentarium Textus Codicis Iuris Canonici,* 6 vols., Lib. IV, *De Processibus,* Romae: Collegio Angelico, 1927.

Bouix, D., *Tractatus de Judiciis Ecclesiasticis,* 3. ed., 2 vols. in 1, Parisiis, 1885.

Buckland, W. W., *The Main Institutions of Roman Private Law,* Cambridge: University Press, 1931.

Coronata, Matthaeus, Conte a, *Institutiones Iuris Canonici,* 3 ed., 5 vols., Taurini et Romae: Marietti, 1947-1951.

Coyle, P. R., *Judicial Exceptions,* The Catholic University of America Canon Law Studies, n. 193, Washington, D. C.: The Catholic University of America Press, 1944.

Clune, R. B., *The Judicial Interrogation of the Parties,* The Catholic University of America Canon Law Studies, n. 269, Washington, D. C.: The Catholic University of America Press, 1948.

Devoti, J., *Iuris Canonici Universi Publici et Privati Libri Quinque,* 3 vols., Romae, 1837.

Dictionnaire de Droit Canonique, 5 vols. and 3 fascicles (incomplete), Paris: Létouzey et Ané, 1924 - -

Giraldi, Ubaldus, *Expositio Iuris Pontificii iuxta Recentiorem Ecclesiae Disciplinam,* 2 vols., Romae: 1769.

Goyeneche, C., *De Processibus,* 2 vols. (pro manuscripto), Romae, 1948.

Hogan, J., *Judicial Advocates and Procurators,* The Catholic University of America Canon Law Studies, n. 133, Washington, D. C.: The Catholic University of America Press, 1941.

Hostiensis, Cardinalis (Henricus de Segusio), *Summa Aurea,* Venetiis, 1570.

Jolowicz, H. F. *Historical Introduction to the Study of Roman Law,* 2. ed., Cambridge: University Press, 1952.

Król, J. J., *The Defendant in Ecclesiastical Trials,* The Catholic University of America Canon Law Studies, n. 146, Washington, D. C.: The Catholic University of America Press, 1942.

Lane, L., *Matrimonial Procedure in the Ordinary Courts of Second Instance,* The Catholic University of America Canon Law Studies, n. 253, Washington, D. C.: The Catholic University of America Press, 1947.

Laurin, Franciscus, *Introductio in Corpus Iuris Canonici,* Friburgi, Brisgoviae et Vindobonae, 1889.

Leage, R. W., *Roman Private Law,* 2. ed., reprint, edited by C. W. Ziegler, London: MacMillan and Company, 1951.

Lega, M., *Praelectiones in Textum Iuris Canonici de Iudiciis Ecclesiasticis,* 4 vols., Romae, 1896 - 1901.

Lega, M. - Bartoccetti, V., *Commentarius in Iudicia Ecclesiastica iuxta Codicem Iuris Canonici,* 2. ed., 3 vols., Romae: Anonima Libraria Cattolica Italiana, 1950.

Manuale delle Fonti del Diritto Romano, 2. edizione per cura di Pietro Cogliolo, Torino, 1911.

Migne, J. P., *Patrologiae Cursus Completus, Series Latina,* 221 vols., Parisiis, 1844-1864.

Muirhead, J., *Historical Introduction to the Private Law of Rome,* 2. ed. revised by H. Goudy, 1899; 3. ed. revised by A. Grant, London: A. and C. Black, Limited, 1916.

Noval, J., *Commentarium Codicis Iuris Canonici, Liber IV, De Processibus,* Pars I, *De Iudiciis,* Romae: Marietti, 1920.

Ottaviani, Alaphridus, *Institutiones Iuris Publici Ecclesiastici,* 3. ed., 2 vols., Civitate Vaticana: Typis Polyglottis Vaticanis, 1947-1948.

Panormitanus, Abbas (Nicolaus de Tudeschis), *Commentaria super Quinque Libros Decretalium,* 5 vols., Venetiis, 1588.

Pinna, J. M., *Praxis Iudicialis Canonica,* Città di Castello: Tipografia della Casa Editrice S. Lapi, 1952.

Pirhing, E., *Ius Canonicum in Quinque Libros Decretalium,* editio novissima, Dilingae, 1722.

Reiffenstuel, Anacletus, *Ius Canonicum Universum,* 5 vols. in 7, Parisiis, 1864-1870.

Roberti, F., *De Processibus,* 2 vols., Romae: Apud Aedes Facultatis Iuridicae ad S. Apollinaris, 1926.

Santi, Franciscus, *Praelectiones Iuris Canonici,* editio quarta emendata et recentissimis decretis accommodata cura M. Leitner, 5 vols. in 2, Ratisbonae, 1903-1905.

Schmalzgrueber, Franciscus, *Ius Ecclesiasticum Universum,* 5 vols. in 12, Romae, 1843-1845.

Scott, S. P., *The Civil Law, a Translation of the Code of Justinian,* 17 vols., Cincinnati: The Central Trust Company, 1932.

Suarez, Franciscus, *Tractatus de Legibus et Legislatore Deo,* Vols. V and VI of the *Opera Omnia,* 28 vols., Parisiis, 1856-1861.

Theodosian Code and Novels, and the Sirmondian Constitutions, a translation by Clyde Pharr, Princeton University Press, 1952.

Traité de Droit Canonique, 4 tomes, publié sous la direction de Raoul Naz, Paris: Létouzey et Ané, 1948 - 1949.

Tuschus, Card., *Practicae Conclusiones Iuris in Omni Foro Frequentiores,* ed. tertia, Tomus 4, Lugduni, 1689.

Van Hove, A., *Commentarium Lovaniense in Codicem Iuris Canonici,* I, *Prolegomena ad Codicem Iuris Canonici,* 2. ed., Mechliniae-Romae: H. Dessain, 1945.

Vermeersch, A.—Creusen, J., *Epitome Iuris Canonici,* 3 vols., Mechliniae-Romae: H. Dessain, Vol. III, 6. ed., 1946.

Wenger, Leopold, *Institutes of the Roman Law of Civil Procedure,* revised edition, New York: Veritas Press, 1940.

Wernz, F. X., *Ius Decretalium ad Usum Praelectionum in Scholis Textus Canonici sive Iuris Decretalium,* 6 vols., Vol. V, Prati, 1914.

Wernz, F. X.—Vidal, P., *Ius Canonicum,* 7 tomes in 8 vols., Romae: Apud Aedes Universitatis Gregorianae, Tom. VI, *De Processibus,* 2. ed., 1949.

Woywod, S.—Smith, C., *A Practical Commentary on the Code of Canon Law,* 2 vols., New York: Joseph F. Wagner, Inc., 1948.

ARTICLES

Berger, Adolph, "Capitis Diminutio." *Encyclopedic Dictionary of Roman Law,* Philadelphia: The American Philosophical Society, 1953.

----------------------------------, "Iudicia Legitima," *Encyclopedic Dictionary of Roman Law,* Philadelphia: The American Philosophical Society, 1953.

----------------------------------, "Translatio Iudicii," *Encyclopedic Dictionary of Roman Law,* Philadelphia: The American Philosophical Society, 1953.

Kuttner, S, "The Father of the Science of Canon Law" — *The Jurist,* Washington, D. C.: The Catholic University of America, I (1941), 2-19.

Ojetti, Benedetto, "Ecclesiastical Courts," — *The Catholic Encyclopedia,* IV, 447-453.

ALPHABETICAL INDEX

Abatement, cf. *Peremptio Acta causae*, 4-6, 51, 63
  and the effects of the *peremptio*, 85-89
  and the effects of the *renuntiatio*, 91-93, 97, 99
Acta processus, 4, 6, 46, 76-81
  and the *Regolamento* of *Gregory* XVI, 32
  and the effects of the *peremptio*, 85-86, 88, 90
  and the effects of the *renuntiatio*, 91-96, 98-100
Action,
  as distinguished from *instantia*, 6. 44-45, 83
  exercise of right of, 6, 43-45
  in personam (personal), 11, 73
  in re (real), 73
  prescription of, 6, 11, 23, 55, 75, 86, 90
  renunciation of the, 29-30, 55-56, 91, 93, 96
  right of, 6, 10-11, 23, 41, 43-45, 54-55, 75, 83, 86, 90, 96, 98-99
Alexander Severus, 8
Appeal, the court of, 3, 22-24, 45, 63, 76-77, 79, 83, 88-90, 92, 96, 98-99
Arbitration, cf. *compromissum in arbitros*
Arcadius, 17
Attentata lite pendente, 57-58
Audientia episcopalis, 17

Benefices, ecclesiastical, litigation over, 36-37, 52, 71-74
  notion of, 72
Bill of complaint, cf. *libellus*
Bologna, University of, 18
Boniface VIII, *Liber Sextus of*, 19, 73

Caesar Augustus, 12
Canon law, medieval study of, 18
Capitis diminutio, notion of, 36
  and the *ius standi in iudicio*, 36
Causa, defined, 2-3
Chalcedon, Council of, 13, 26
Citatio, 1-3, 12, 51, 59-61, 67, 74, 80-82
  as a procedural act, 42, 86, 90
Clement V, 19
  and litigation over benefices, 36
Clement VIII, the Constitution *Litium* of, 25
Clementinae, 19
Code of Justinian, 14, 18, 28
Cognitio, 8-9, 12
Collatio, libera, 72
Commission for the Authentic Interpretation of the Code, 92-93
Compositio, 52
Compromissum in arbitros, notion of. 53
  as concluding the *instantia*, 53-54, 56
Conclusio in causa, 1. 57-60. 62-63. 67-71
Concordia, 52
Constantine, 13, 17
Constitution,
  Ad Romani of Gregory XIII, 25
  Litium of Clement VIII, 25
Constitutions (Novels) of Justinian. 14, 18
Contumacy, 22, 51, 56, 61-62, 71
Coronata, 43-45, 55, 62, 69, 82, 85
Corpus Iuris Canonici, 1, 19
Corpus Iuris Civilis, 1, 14
Court costs,
  in contumacious proceedings, 51
  in Justinian legislation, 15-16
  in the *peremptio*, 90, 99-100
  in the *renuntiatio*, 29, 32, 38, 99-100
  in the *transactio*, 52

Decretalists, 2, 5
Decretals, 1, 5, 40
  and litigation over benefices, 36
  interpretation of the, 20-21
  modification and change under the, 19-23
  of Gregory IX, 19, 24
Decretum Gratiani, 19
Defender of the Bond, 67, 98
Dictionnaire de Droit Canonique, 61
Digest of Justinian, 14, 18
Diocletian, 12
Dominate, era of the, 12, 14

Edict of Milan, 17
Equity, rules of, 53
Exceptions, judicial, 54-55, 57, 65, 71, 81, 84-85
  peremptory, 54, 81, 84-85
  dilatory, 54
  as concluding the *instantia,* 54-55, 81, 84-85
Excommunication, and the *ius standi in iudicio,* 36, 64-66, 71
Extravagantes, of John XXII, 19
  Communes, 19

Formula, notion of the, 8-10, 12
  abolition of system of the, 12

Gaius, 9-11, 27
Germanic invasions, 18-19
Giraldi, 24-26
Glossators, 19
Glosses, 19, 21
Gratian, *Decretum* of, 18-19
Gregory I, 17
Gregory IX, Decretals of, 19
Gregory XIII, the Constitution *Ad Romani* of, 25
Gregory XVI, and litigation over ecclesiastical benefices, 37
  and the *Lex Propria* of 1908, 33
  and the *Regulae Servandae,* 33
  judiciary rules (*Regolamento*) of, 31-32, 37
Guardians, 64, 66, 69-71, 81-82, 98

Heir in the judicial cause, 58-63, 67
Honorius III, the *Venerabilis Frater* of, 19-21, 23-24

Impediment, legitimate to proceedings, 59, 76-79, 82
Imperium of magistrates, The, 10
Insanity, and the *ius standi in iudicio,* 36, 64, 98
Instantia, cf. *Litis instantia*
Institutes of Justinian, The, 14
Interrogation, the judicial, 46
Interruptio instantiae, and ecclesiastical benefices, 71-74
  and the *ius standi in iudicio,* 35-37
  causes productive of the, 59-71
  effects of the, 38, 57-58
  influence on the *peremptio* of, 27, 78, 82
  notion of the, 34, 38, 57-58
  Roman law and the, 35
Irnerius, 18
Iudicia, legitima, 9-12
  imperio continentia, 9-12
Iudicium, 2-3, 39-41
  and the termination of the *instantia,* 49-51
Iusiurandum decisorium, notion of the, 52-53
  as concluding the *instantia,* 52-53, 56
Ius patronatus, 72
Ius standi in iudicio,
  and the *capitis diminutio,* 36
  and the *res iudicata,* 45
  and the *translatio iudicii,* 35, 37
  effect of death on the, 37, 62-63
  effect of excommunication on the, 36, 64-66
  effect of insanity on the, 36, 64
  in litigation over ecclesiastical benefices, 36-37, 71-74
  in the *interruptio instantiae,* 34-37, 57-60, 63-66
  in the suspension of a cause, 34, 57-58
  of minors, 64, 78
  of religious, 64

John XXII, The *Extravagantes* of, 19, 73
Joinder of issue, cf. *Litis contestatio*
Juridical status of parties in trial, cf. *ius standi in iudicio*
Justinian, 3, 13-15, 18, 20-23, 25, 27, 30

Lega-Bartoccetti, 45, 80, 82, 88, 94
Leges Iuliae, 9
Legis actio, characteristics of the, 8-9
Lex Aebutia, 8-9
Lex Properandum, 3, 14-16
  and the *Venerabilis Frater*, 20-21
Lex Propria of the Rota, 31-33
Lex Romana, 18
Libellus, 1-4, 48, 55-56, 60
  as a procedural act, 42, 46, 86
Liber Sextus of Boniface VIII, The, 19
Limitation, Statute of, 15, 23, 26
Lis, 2-3
Litigation, over benefices, 36-37, 71-74
  per certa verba, 9
  per concepta verba, 9
Litis contestatio, 1-4, 9, 39-40, 42, 46-47
  and judicial exceptions, 54
  and the Council of Trent, 24
  and the *interruptio instantiae*, 60, 68, 71
  and the *Lex Properandum*, 20
  and the *litis instantia*, 47-48, 74, 80-81, 94-95
  and the *renuntiatio*, 94-96
  and the *translatio iudicii*, 35
  and the *Venerabilis Frater*, 20-21
  the equivalent of the, 48
Litis instantia,
  after Honorius III, 23-24
  after the Council of Trent, 25
  and law of Justinian, 14, 23
  and the *interruptio*, 34, 36, 57-74
  and the *peremptio*, 49, 75-90
  and the *renuntiatio*, 49, 91-100
  and the *res iudicata*, 43-44
  as distinguished from the *actio*, 6, 44-45
  as distinguished from the *processus*, 39-46
  as modified by custom, 26-27
  as the sequel to the *litis contestatio*, 47-48
  defined, 1-2, 39-46
  inception of the, 46-48, 80-81
  in later Roman law, 12
  in the practice of the Rota, 26
  position in judicial process, 2, 39, 46-56
  resumption of the, 60-61, 68, 71
  termination of the, 48-56
  understanding the, 38

Minors, Status of, 64, 78, 81-83, 98
Moral personality, A, 62, 66-67, 98

Normae of the Rota, 83
Noval, 43-45, 50, 92
Novels (Constitutions) of Justinian, The, 14, 18

Oath, Decisive, cf. *iusiurandum decisorium*
Office, Ecclesiastical, 69-70, 72
  conferment of, 72-73
  election to, 72-73
  nomination to, 72-73
  presentation to, 72-73

Panormitanus, 21
Peremptio instantiae,
  affinity to the *renuntiatio instantiae*, 29-30, 38, 76-77, 88, 91-93, 96, 99-100
  after the Germanic invasions, 18
  and the *interruptio instantiae*, 58, 82
  and the prescription of an action, 6, 11, 75
  and the termination of the *instantia*, 49, 56
  and the *Venerabilis Frater*, 21-23
  conditions productive of the, 76-81
  defined, 4, 6-7, 75-76
  development from the Council of Trent, 23-27

dilatory tactics in the, 15, 19-20
effects of the, 38, 42, 85-90
historical precedents, 7-11
in Justinian legislation, 14-15, 20
in the 12th and 13th centuries, 19, 28
persons affected by the, 81-85
vicissitudes of the, 27-28
Petition, A judicial, 3
Pinna, 68-69
Pisa, 18
Postulation, 72
Praescriptio actionis, 6, 11, 23, 55, 90
and the *peremptio instantiae*, 6, 11, 75, 86, 90
and the *renuntiatio instantiae*, 99
Praxis processualis, 26-28, 34, 83
Principate, era of the, 12
Proceedings,
apud iudicem, 9
in iure, 9
Processus, iudiciarius, 2-3, 39-46, 49-50, 75, 81, 86, 95
Procurator, cf. Proxy
Promoter of Justice, 67, 71, 73-74, 98
Proofs, documentary, 59, 85-87, 97, 99
Properandum, lex, 3, 14-16
and the *Venerabilis Frater*, 20-22
Proxy, 57-59, 62, 64, 81-82
as renouncing the *instantia*, 31, 96, 98-99
ius standi in iudicio of the, 34-35, 37, 66-71

Quaestio, defined, 3
Questiones, incidental, 45, 52, 55, 58, 60, 87

Ravenna, archbishop of, 20
Regolamento of Gregory XVI, 32-33
and the *ius standi in iudicio*, 37
Regulae Iuris of Boniface VIII, 5
Regulae Servandae of Roman Rota, 31-33
and the *res iudicata*, 33
as elaboration of the *Lex Propria*, 33
Reiffenstuel, 1-3, 26, 42, 44, 55
Religious, status of, 64, 70
Renuntiatio instantiae,
affinity to the *peremptio instantiae*, 29-30, 38, 76-77, 88, 91-93, 96. 99-100
and the termination of the *instantia*, 49, 56, 88, 91-96
development in ecclesiastical procedure, 31-34
effects of the, 99-100
formalities in the, 96-99
notion and indications in ancient law, 29-30
Renunciation of a *peremptio instantiae*, 85
Renunciation of the *acta processus*, 30-34, 91-96
Renunciation of the action, 29-30, 55-56, 93
Res iudicata,
and the juridical status of persons. 45
and the *litis instantia*, 43-45, 83
and the *peremptio instantiae*, 77, 83, 88-90
and the *Regolamento* of Gregory XVI, 32
and the *Regulae Servandae* of the Rota, 33
and the *renuntiatio instantiae*, 96, 98-99
effects of the, 38
influence in modern Church law, 32
Restitutio in integrum,
and the *peremptio instantiae*, 82-84
in Roman law, 12
Roberti, 41-43, 50, 68-69, 94
Roman empire,
autocratic, 12
division of eras in the, 12
Roman law,
and ecclesiastical courts, 13, 17-18, 21
and the *interruptio instantiae*, 35-36
and the *ius standi in iudicio*, 37
and the *peremptio instantiae*, 8, 27, 75-76

and the *renuntiatio instantiae*, 30
basic notions of, 8-11, 40
growth of substantive law in, 9
renaissance of, 18
Rota, Sacred Roman, 26-27, 60
decisions of the, 26-27, 63
Lex Propria of the, 31-32
procedural practice of the, 26-27, 34, 83-84
Regulae Servandae of the, 31-32

Sacred Roman Rota, cf. Rota
Sententia, 2
and the *litis instantia*, 43-46, 48-49, 55, 63, 65, 88
and the *renuntiatio instantiae*, 33
execution of the, 49-51
interlocutory, 87-89
Simple compromise, cf. *Transactio*
Successor to the judicial cause, 58-62, 67
Summary causes, 5
Summons, cf. *Citatio*
Suspension of the *instantia*, 34, 57-58

Theodosian Code, 26
Theodosius II, 13
Transactio,
as terminating the *instantia*, 52, 56
nature of the, 51-52, 56
Translatio iudicii,
and the *ius standi in iudicio*, 37
nature of the, 35, 37
Trent, Council of, 23
ruling in the *peremptio* of the, 23-26, 28
Twelve Tables, Roman law of the, 30

Valentinian III, 17
Venerabilis Frater of Honorius III, 19
and the law of *peremptio*, 21-23
and the *lex Properandum*, 20-21
interpretation of the, 21
Vidal, 43-45, 82
Visigoths, 18

Wenger, 35
Wernz, 35

BIOGRAPHICAL NOTE

Albert William Olkovikas was born on September 12, 1927, in Manchester, New Hampshire. He received his elementary and secondary education there in the parochial schools of Saint Joseph's Parish. From June, 1945, to May, 1947, he attended Saint Thomas' Seminary in Bloomfield, Connecticut. He made his philosophical studies at the *Séminaire de Philosophie* in Montreal, from which he entered the *Grand Séminaire de Montréal* in 1949. He received the degree of Baccalaureate of Sacred Theology in June, 1952 and the Licentiate of Sacred Theology in May, 1953. He was ordained to the priesthood for the Diocese of Manchester on May 30 of that year and served as assistant to Saint Anthony's Parish, Sanbornville, New Hampshire, during the summer of 1953. He entered the School of Canon Law at the Catholic University of America in October, 1953, and was awarded the degree of Bachelor of Canon Law in June, 1954, and the degree of Licentiate of Canon Law in June, 1955.

CANON LAW STUDIES*

368. Bockstie, Rev. Richard, C.Ss.R., J.C.L., The principal oratory of religious.

369. Grajewski, Rev. Maurice J., O.F.M., M.A., Ph.D., J.C.L., The supreme moderator of exempt religious orders.

370. Havlik, Rev. Bernard J., A.B., J.C.L., The cessation of rescripts.

371. Olkovikas, Rev. Albert William, S.T.L., J.C.L., The *instantia* of the lawsuit.

372. Poblete, Rev. Elias Olarte, J.C.L., The plenary council.

373. Sokolich, Rev. Alexander F., S.T.L., J.C.L., Canonical provisions for universities and colleges.

374. Sullivan, Rev. Jordan J., O.F.M. Cap., B.A., J.C.L., Fast and abstinence in the First Order of St. Francis.

* For a complete list of the available numbers of this series apply to the Catholic University of America Press, 620 Michigan Ave., N.E., Washington (17), D. C., for general catalog.

www.ingramcontent.com/pod-product-compliance
Lightning Source LLC
LaVergne TN
LVHW050204080826
844660LV00012B/352
9780813225333